Railway Memor

The travels of a Yorkshi
Newspaper photograph

SKIPTON

B

Compiled by Alan C Butcher

The
Transport
Treasury

The Transport Treasury

Reviving the memories of yesterday…

© Images and design: The Transport Treasury 2021. Text Alan C Butcher.

ISBN 978-1-913251-13-0

First published in 2021 by Transport Treasury Publishing Ltd., 16 Highworth Close, High Wycombe, HP13 7PJ

www.ttpublishing.co.uk

Printed in the UK by Henry Ling Limited at the Dorset Press, Dorchester. DT1 1HD

Front cover: Striding purposefully towards the cameraman, one traveller is happy for his photograph to be taken. The train locomotive, Thompson Class B1 4-6-0 No. 61387 has arrived at Leeds Central's platform 4 with an express service. Built by the North British Locomotive Co in November 1951. No. 61387 was shedded at 37B (Copley Hill, Leeds), surviving until October 1965. Opened as a joint station between the LNWR, L&YR, GNR and NER in 1854, Leeds Central replaced a cramped MR terminus at Leeds Wellington (opened 1 July 1846). The last train left Central on Saturday 29 April; as there was no Sunday service, formal closure came on 1 May 1967 when all services were concentrated at Leeds City. *Ref:1222.*

Rear cover: The privately operated Derwent Valley Light Railway ran from York, Layerthorpe Road, to Cliffe Common near Selby on the now closed Selby-Market Weighton route; it was unusual in that it was never Nationalised. Latterly the line hired motive power from BR and a Class 03 0-6-0DM No. 2112 was one of the 204hp Class 03 0-6-0DMs built at Doncaster between November 1958 and December 1960. The overgrown state of the track is clearly visible; a feature of a lot of light railways, rendering them almost invisible in aerial photographs which was an advantage during World War 2 as they would not be visible in enemy reconnaissance photographs. *Ref:1913.*

Frontispiece: During the early 1950s BR were looking to reduce operating costs, and as a result several thousand diesel multiple-units were introduced. These were built not only in BR's main workshops, but also by private contractors. The Class 108 units, a two-car set is seen here, were built at Derby Works from 1958 to 1960. Officialdom have met the driver on arrival at Skipton – did he do something wrong? Note the trollies on the platform, at this time BR still carried parcels on passenger trains; the service, latterly known as Red Star Parcels continued until January 1999 when it was sold to Lynx Express, who in turn were taken over by UPS in 2005. Red Star's rail based service ceased operations in 2001. *Ref:1418.*

Opposite: Gresley 'A3' class No 60086 *Gainsborough* emerged from Doncaster Works in April 1930 as No. 2597. It was named after the racehorse that won the English Triple Crown in 1918; the horse was named after the town of Gainsborough, Lincolnshire, because his owner liked the sound of the name. No 60086 is seen here leaving York in the snow; it was withdrawn in November 1963. *Ref:1855.*

Copies of the illustrations can be obtained from The Transport Treasury (address above) by quoting 'Glass Plate Negatives Miscellany' list along with the appropriate reference / page number.

Contents

Above: In 1927 the London Midland & Scottish Railway chose to name the first of its new class of 4-6-0 express locomotives after British regiments. No. 6100 was named after the Royal Scots (The Royal Regiment), once known as the Royal Regiment of Foot, being the oldest and most senior infantry regiment of the line of the British Army, having been raised in 1633 during the reign of Charles I of Scotland.

Six years later in 1933, No 6152 *The King's Dragoon Guardsman* and the original No. 6100 swapped identities permanently. No. 6152 had been built at Derby Works in 1930. The 'new' *Royal Scot* was sent to the Century of Progress Exposition of 1933 and toured Canada and the United States with a train of typical LMS carriages. It was shipped partially disassembled aboard the Canadian Pacific Steamship Co. ship SS Beaverdale. Some years later in 1941 the ship was torpedoed by U-boat U-48, with 21 of its crew being killed. The Master, Captain Draper, navigated one lifeboat 300 miles to Iceland the other lifeboat being rescued at sea.

Following the tour No 6100 was given special commemorative plates that sit below its nameplates. Following nationalisation, in 1948, it was renumbered 46100. In 1950 it was rebuilt with a taper boiler, and the words 'Prior to conversion' were added to its commemorative plates. It was withdrawn from service in Nottingham and purchased by Billy Butlin of holiday camp fame. Following eight years on display at Skegness it was relocated to Bressingham Steam Museum in Norfolk. Now owned by the Royal Scot Locomotive & General Trust, a charitable trust set up in 2009, it has operated steam-hauled trips on the main line. *Ref:1256.*

Opposite: The South East Leeds Conservative Party on a day trip stand in front of one of the Gresley-designed beaver-tail saloons at Leeds station. There were two of these carriages designed in 1935 for the launch of the LNER's 'Coronation' express that ran from London Kings Cross to Edinburgh. The service was inaugurated on 5 July 1937 and ran until the start of World War 2 when the coaches were put into store. In 1948 various vehicles returned to service as general passenger stock; they never ran as a full set again – the observation cars were transferred to the West Highland line in 1956. *Ref:1520.*

Introduction

It is late spring 1758 and Parliament has a decision to make that will, ultimately, make a fundamental change to the countryside and change the world forever. On 9 June the Middleton Railway was the first to be sanctioned by an Act of Parliament. It gave its owner and promoter – Charles Brandling – authority to run his tracks over other owners' lands using a system of way leaves. He had sought the Act as security to secure his future rights to maintain and operate the railway. The first line was of 4ft 1in gauge and of wooden construction. Using horsepower the first load of coal arrived at Casson Close, Leeds, on 26 September 1758. The West Riding of Yorkshire had all the prerequisites of industry – stone to build factories (and back-to-back housing), coal and fast flowing streams to provide power and iron to construct machinery – leading to the industrial revolution. The first railway, in the modern sense, to be incorporated in the region was the Leeds & Selby Railway of 1830. Its genesis was the success of the Stockton & Darlington Railway in 1825 and the subsequent promotion of the Liverpool & Manchester Railway. The subsequent 'railway mania' resulted in links to all points of the compass, bringing in raw materials and transporting coal and manufactured goods around the country, and ultimately the world.

The depression of the 1920s caused the railway network to suffer initial rationalisation, which accelerated after World War 2 with the rise of road transport. In the early 1960s Dr Richard Beeching promoted his vision on the 'modernisation of Britain's railways' that resulted in mass closure of lines over the following years.

The images used in this title originally formed part of a newspaper archive. Whether the photographer was a member of staff or a freelance is not known, it is evident that he was an enthusiast as not all are always 'newsworthy'. A number of images were taken on visits to parts of 'Greater' Yorkshire and are included for their interest in adding to the overall story. The majority are taken in the 1950s or early 1960s. Little information was available with the images so recourse has been made to the internet and books listed in the Bibliography for much of the text and caption detail. My thanks to those who make this information freely available.

ACB, Dereham, Summer 2021

Chapter 1

Stations

Arthington

There have been two stations at Arthington. The first was opened on 10 April 1849 by the Leeds & Thirsk Railway (becoming the Leeds Northern Railway on 3 July 1851). Originally known as Pool, it was renamed in September 1852. The second station seen here was built to serve the Otley branch that opened on 1 February 1865, superseding the first station, being some 900ft to the south. The two sides of the railway triangle that lay to the north and west have been dismantled (the west curve closed 22 March 1965 to passenger traffic and and 5 July to freight; northern curve closed 25 February 1957 to passengers). Trains still pass the eastern part of the triangle on the Harrogate line.

Above: Photographed early in 1965, with the Station Master posing for posterity, this view was taken to record the scene shortly before closure which occurred on 22 March 1965. *Ref:2243.*

Left: No doubt about the location, the station sign was probably taken on the same date as the main image. It was reported in the *Ilkley Gazette* in April 2014 that it was proposed to re-open the station to alleviate road traffic into Leeds along the parallel 'A' class roads. However, the West Yorkshire Combined Authority declined to push forward with the plans for 'Arthington Parkway'. In 2017 the transport secretary invited proposals from local authorities who believed they had a business case to reopen lines and stations. In 2021 the residents of Arthington are still await the reopening of their station. *Ref:2479.*

Stations

Barnby Dun

This was a small station on the South Yorkshire Railway's line between Doncaster and Thorne in South Yorkshire. The original line followed closely the canal bank with the station opening on 7 July 1857. The station, closed on 1 October 1866, was resited when the line was 'straightened', with the new station being sited at the opposite side of the village. The station was again rebuilt to accommodate four tracks in the Doncaster to Thorne widening of 1913. The rebuilt station remained operational for passenger traffic until 4 September 1967; goods traffic ceased on 5 April 1965.

Most railway companies and later the BR regions operated a 'Best Station' competition. Barnby Dun was entered and the Station Master is seen here showing his staffs' efforts at gardening. *Ref:1710.*

Ben Rhydding

The station was built as part of the Otley & Ilkley Joint Railway, and opened to passenger traffic on 1 July 1866, some 11 months after the opening of the railway in the village of Wheatley. In the 19th century Wheatley was noted for its hydropathic establishment that opened on 29 March 1844 at a cost of £30,000. Ben Rhydding, the name given to the establishment, was also given to the railway station built to serve it and by which the village subsequently became known. In April 1865 the North Eastern Railway Board ordered 'that a small wooden station consisting of booking office, waiting room and retiring room for ladies be provided as a temporary accommodation at Ben Rhydding'. Six years later, in May 1871, the Joint Committee reached an agreement with the proprietor of the Ben Rhydding Hydro, that a more permanent station structure should be built at the expense of the Hydro, with a ground rent of a penny (0.5p) per annum, so long as the structures met the approval of the railway engineer. The Hydro's arrangements with the company lasted until 1885, when the structures – a stone built station house on the south platform and a wooden structure on the north platform – were sold to the railway company for £240. Goods traffic ceased on 5 July 1965, and the sidings later removed. The introduction of 'pay-trains' resulted in the station staff being withdrawn on 7 October 1968. Regretfully the unusual station building has subsequently been demolished, and shelter on both platforms is restricted to simple bus-stop type covered areas.

Above: The station staff pose outside the station at 4pm, the date is not recorded, though probably taken at the same occasion. Today's station is but a shadow of its former self with a small car park but no other amenities. There is however an extensive timetable with regular services to Leeds, Bradford and Ilkley. *Ref:2440.*

Opposite: A Metro-Cammell Class 101 DMU arrives at the station in April 1963 from Ilkley. Metropolitan-Cammell of Washford Heath in Birmingham was the largest provider of diesel multiple-units to British Railways. The Class 101 low-density units were some of the most successful, and long-lived, of the first generation units. Introduced in 1956 numerous examples were still in service at the start of the 21st century. *Ref:2259.*

Bradford Exchange

The original L&YR station, opened 9 May 1850, but with inadequate passenger facilities it was closed on 7 January 1867 when the line was extended to Exchange station, that was closer to the city centre near to the wool exchange, after which it was named. The rapid growth of traffic resulted in the first rebuilding taking place by the end of the 1870s. It was operated by the L&YR and GNR, each having independent platforms and booking offices, an arrangement that continued until January 1940. Following World War 2 traffic declined to an extent that by 1973 it was decided that 10 platforms were too large for the volume of traffic. The ex-L&YR platforms were taken of service to permit the construction of the first two platforms of the new station – situated to the south of the Bridge Street bridge (the failure of which was one cause of the relocation). With the completion of the first two platforms, the ex-GNR platforms were taken out of use on 14 January 1973; this permitted the construction of the additional two platforms. The platforms of Interchange station were built on the original running lines out of Exchange. The adjacent bus station and underground bus depot were built on the site of the Bridge Street goods shed. The station was officially renamed Interchange in 1983 and the site of the old station is now occupied by the law courts although traces of the old building can still be seen.

Derby Lightweight vehicle No 79511 (a Driving Motor Composite) leaves the station. The turntable served a servicing area, dating from the late 1800s it survived until the end of steam in the area. It was situated very close to a running line, so care would be needed when turning a locomotive. *Ref:1540.*

Bridlington

The station was opened on 6 October 1846 by the York & North Midland Railway as the terminus of their line running from Hull. An extension northwards to Filey leading to a junction at Seamer station, connecting with the York to Scarborough line, was opened just over a year later. The station was extended after World War 1 to cater for the increasing excursion traffic with through trains to Leeds, London and the Midlands. In July 1958, Class D49 No. 62703 *Hertfordshire* ran into the turntable pit and rolled onto its side. By the mid-1960s traffic had declined and rationalisation followed. The station was designated a Grade II listed building in 2003 and is now recorded in the National Heritage List for England, maintained by Historic England. In the summer of 2019 work commenced on a multi-million pound scheme to transform the station entrance.

Built by the North Eastern Railway at Darlington in December 1919, this three-cylinder Class B16/1 No. 61471 survived in traffic until September 1960. Note the enamel Virol advertisement sign below the station name board. Virol was a by-product of the brewing industry packed full of nutrients, malt, sugar and vitamins such as riboflavin. Due to its concentrated nutritious content, Virol was been heavily marketed for anaemic girls, growing boys, and delicate children. It disappeared from the shelves post 1980. *Ref:2092.*

Castle Howard

Situated on the still open York to Scarborough line, the station here served the village of Welburn and was opened on 5 July 1845 by the York & North Midland Railway. It was named after the nearby Castle Howard, and often used by the aristocracy, notably Queen Victoria and Prince Albert as guests of the Earl of Carlisle in August 1850. An early closure to passenger traffic, on 22 September 1930, it remained staffed until 2 November 1950 to handle small volumes of goods traffic.

With signs of dereliction all around the final closure has occurred; the station building survives as holiday accommodation. The station featured in the TV serial 'Brideshead Revisited' in 1981 and the 2008 film of the same name; it was also featured in the TV programme 'The Architecture the Railways Built', series 1, episode 6 during 2020. *Ref:1622.*

Clapham

The station was opened by the 'little' North Western Railway (NWR) on 30 July 1849 on their line from Skipton to Ingleton and became a junction the following year when the link along the Wenning valley from Bentham was completed on 1 June 1850 to finish the route from Lancaster to Skipton. The Ingleton route was subsequently extended northwards, as the Ingleton branch line, through Kirkby Lonsdale and Sedbergh to join the West Coast main line at Low Gill (near Tebay) by the Lancaster & Carlisle Railway (L&C) in 1861. Disagreements between the L&C's successor, the London & North Western Railway, and the Midland Railway (who had leased the NWR in 1859) over running rights, and the subsequent construction of the Settle-Carlisle line, meant that it never became the major Anglo-Scottish route that the NWR had originally intended. The Ingleton branch was closed to passenger traffic on 1 February 1954 and completely in July 1966, although regular goods traffic had ended some months earlier. Lifting of the track followed in April 1967. Clapham station ceased to handle goods traffic on 25 January 1965, when the remaining sidings were taken out of use and dismantled and the signal box closed.

Stanier Class 5XP No. 45658 *Keyes* is seen in the snow at Clapham station. Built at Derby in December 1934 the locomotive survived in traffic until October *1965. Ref:1889.*

Stations

Damems

This is a station on the Worth Valley line between Keighley and Oxenhope; funded predominantly by local wealthy mill owners it opened on 15 April 1867; with the halt at Damens opening on 1 September. The line was operated by the Midland Railway from opening; officially leased in 1876 it was formally absorbed in 1881, becoming part of the LMS at the Grouping. Upon Nationalisation in 1948, the line became part of British Railways, and with its fortunes declining with the rise of competition from the roads, the branch closed in 1962. All traffic at Damems ceased on 23 May 1949 shortly after these photographs were taken on 17 March. Today Damems survives as a station on the heritage Keighley & Worth Valley Railway that reopened on 29 June 1968. The railway is perhaps most famous for its role in the 1970 film version of Edith Nesbit's story 'The Railway Children'. *Ref:2519.*

As can be seen in these images the platform is only long enough for one coach, that makes this the smallest 'full-size' station in Britain; and the station house is situated to the opposite side of the track. From 1928 the station house was occupied by Mrs Annie Feather, who was responsible for operating the level crossing gates by hand. The signals were operated by a ground frame situated in the front garden. The station closed to passengers in 1949, but Annie continued until the line closed and even then would occasionally work the gates and signals for some of the first trains operated by the K&WVR. See kwvr.co.uk for additional information on how the station appears today. *Ref:2530.*

Dore & Totley

The station was opened by the Midland Railway, for passengers only, as Dore & Totley on 1 February 1872 on the then two-year-old Midland main line extension from Chesterfield to Sheffield, and was initially served by the local services on this line. Six or seven weekday trains and three on Sundays then served the station. In 1894 the station became the junction for the new Dore and Chinley line (now known as the Hope Valley Line).

Dore & Totley Station Junction was at the south end of the station and the signal box stood in the angle between the Chesterfield and Chinley lines. Between 1901 and 1902, the line between Sheffield station and Dore was widened; the original twin tracks continued to be used by traffic for the Dore and Chinley line and two new tracks were built to the east of this for traffic on the main line to Chesterfield. The original southbound platform was converted to an island platform and a new platform for trains to Chesterfield built to the east. The line from Chesterfield was slewed into its present course to serve the new platforms.
A replacement Dore & Totley Station Junction was made to the north of the station. Subsequent rationalisation saw the station reduced to a single platform and it became south Sheffield's only remaining station after the Beeching cuts in the 1960s saw Beauchief, Millhouses and Heeley stations all close. The station's main line platforms were closed to traffic and it became an unstaffed halt in 1969. It was renamed Dore on 18 March 1971 until April 2008 when the full name was restored. *Ref:2463.*

Durham

Opposite: The image is dated 13 July 1944, and is looking down North Road towards the Castle; the spire seen through the left hand arch is of Our Lady of Mercy & St Godric's Church. Durham station is off to the left. The city of Durham was over the years served by four stations. Taking them in chronological order: Shincliffe (called Shincliffe Town from 1861) was located in nearby Shincliffe, opened on 28 June 1839 by the Durham & Sunderland Railway, and used rope haulage until 1856. It closed, in 1893, when Elvet station opened, on 24 July 1893, in the city centre. A second station, Shincliffe, on the Leamside to Ferryhill line, was opened on 19 June 1844; it closed to passengers on 28 July 1941 with final closure to goods traffic on 11 November 1963. Durham (Gilesgate), opened on 15 April 1844, was within the city boundaries, and was served by a branch from Belmont on the Leamside line, then the main line from London to Newcastle. Passenger services finished on 1 April 1857 with the opening of the current station on the branch from Leamside to Bishop Auckland but it continued in use as a goods yard until final closure in 1966. A final station opened on 1 January 1857, being on the current location, and viaducts over North Road and the River Browney immediately to the south were built by the NER, on their Leamside to Bishop Auckland line. The station was redeveloped in 1871, when the NER developed a new line from Tursdale through Relly Mill Junction to Durham, and onwards from Newton Hall Junction through Chester-le-Street to Newcastle Central via the Team Valley. This became the main line, the current East Coast main line, on 15 January 1872. Durham (Elvet) opened on 24 July 1893; the Durham-Sunderland branch was diverted from Shincliffe Town to a new station at Elvet, within the city boundary. It closed to regular passenger services on 1 January 1931 and fully closed on 11 January 1954. BR withdrew passenger services to Bishop Auckland and Sunderland via Penshaw under the Beeching cuts, on 4 May 1964. *Ref:1538.*

Garsdale

On the famed Settle & Carlisle line the station serves the immediate hamlet of Garsdale Head and the nearby towns of Sedburgh and Hawes. The cottages seen in the view were built for the use of railway workers; the station opened as Hawes Junction on 1 August 1876, with the opening of what is now known as the Wensleydale line through Hawes, Redmire and Leyburn. The station was subsequently renamed Hawes Junction & Garsdale on 20 January 1900; a further renaming took place on 1 September 1931 – becoming Garsdale. Following the general rationalisation of the railway network the station closed on 4 May 1970. Following a concerted effort to save the Settle & Carlisle line, the station reopened on 14 July 1986. In the days of steam-hauled London-Scotland expresses, the locality once boasted the highest water troughs in the world (south of the station at Ling Gill). Unusually, the station waiting room was once used for Anglican Church services. *Ref:1150.*

Goathland and Grosmont

These stations together with Levisham, are now on the heritage North Yorkshire Moors Railway. The line was declared to be uneconomic and closed to freight traffic on 27 April 1964 with passenger traffic ceasing on 8 March 1965. The line was reopened between Pickering and Grosmont on 22 April 1973 as a heritage attraction.

Goathland

Opposite top: This station (originally known as Goathland Mill) is on the deviation line opened by the NER in 1865 to avoid the cable-worked Beck Hole Incline, which was part of the original 1836 Whitby & Pickering Railway route. The original Goathland station was located at the head of the incline, where there are still some Y&NM cottages, together with a single W&P one. The station buildings were to the design of the NER's architect Thomas Prosser and were very similar to those being built concurrently (by the same contractor, Thomas Nelson) on the Castleton to Grosmont section of the Esk Valley Line at Danby, Lealholm, Glaisdale and Egton. The collection of buildings is very little altered since they were built – the last recorded change (apart from NYMR restoration) was in 1908. Goathland is well known for its television and film appearances – 'Aidensfield' in Heartbeat; as 'Hogsmeade' in the Harry Potter films; 'Mannerton' in the original BBC television series *All Creatures Great and Small*. *Ref:1704.*

Grosmont

Opposite bottom: The Whitby & Pickering Railway arrived in Grosmont in 1835 with the station opening on 8 June as Tunnel Inn; the line initially being horse-worked. In 1845 the railway was sold to the Y&NMR; with additional parliamentary powers obtained (by the W&P) to make various improvements to its alignment and to permit the introduction of steam power; with the line being converted from single into a fully double tracked steam-powered railway; with the first steam locomotive entering Whitby in July 1847. At Grosmont a new station was built, creating the town's first true station as seen here. The line between Whitby and Middlesbrough via Castleton and Battersby is operated as the Esk Valley Line. *Ref:170.*

Halifax Town

The original station to serve the town was built at Shaw Syke, slightly to the west of the current station; the Manchester & Leeds Railway opened the station seen here on 7 August 1850. It was rebuilt and enlarged in the mid-1880s, and was renamed Halifax Old in June 1890. The new station had separate facilities for L&YR and GNR services. The name change was to distinguish it from the town's St Paul's and North Bridge stations. A further name change to Halifax Town occurred on 30 September 1951. A final change to Halifax took place on 12 June 1961. The station site at Shaw Syke was extended and used as a goods depot.The images here illustrate (left) the arrival of a a Hughes/Fowler 2-6-0, and (opposite) a Stanier Class 5MT 4-6-0 No. 44930, both on three coach trains from Bradford. *Ref:2229 (right), 2339 (opposite).*

Hayburn Wyke

Above: Hayburn Wyke station was on the Scarborough & Whitby Railway, a late arrival on the scene, opening on 16 July 1885 – almost 40 years after the first proposal to connect the two seaside towns; the topography and lack of funds contributing to the delay. Hayburn Wyke, some seven miles from Scarborough, opened with the line and served the popular beauty spot and its hotel. The station was rebuilt in 1893, and closed temporarily (as a wartime economy) on 1 March 1917. Reopening took place on 2 May 1921, before final, permanent closure on 8 March 1965. From 1955 the station was reduced to an unstaffed halt, and it is probably after this date that LNER Class A8 No. 69885 was photographed as it called at the station. Originally built by the NER at Darlington as 4-4-4Ts, the entire class was rebuilt by the LNER between 1931 and 1936 as 4-6-2Ts. The last examples were withdrawn in 1960. The route survives as the Scarborough to Whitby Trailway, a cycleway and footpath. *Ref:1508.*

Stations

Holbeck

Holbeck station was opened by the Leeds, Bradford & Halifax Junction Railway, on 2 July 1855, almost a year after the other stations were opened on the line. It was unusual in that it had platforms on two different levels, with High Level being a joint Great Northern Railway and Lancashire & Yorkshire Railway venture and Low Level – a joint Midland and North Eastern Railway venture. British Railways added the designations of High Level and Low Level in 1951. Holbeck was a cramped station and suffered from trains awaiting paths into the various Leeds termini after being held at junctions on the approaches to and from Leeds. Passengers on the Midland/NER lines would simply stay on the train and change to another service at Wellington station. The reduction in use accelerated the demise of Holbeck station on 7 July 1958 – well before the Beeching closures affected the other stations on the lines that it served. The route on which trains ran through Holbeck High Level station to Leeds Central station closed in 1967, with the tracks subsequently being lifted and the bridge carrying the high level track over the low level removed.

Opposite top: A Metro-Cammell three-car unit stands at the High Level platforms *Ref:1250.*

Opposite bottom: A view along the platforms at Low Level. The chimneys, seen above the High Level bridge, belong to the Monk Bridge Iron & Steel Works. In July 1866 the company was registered to take over the Monk Bridge Iron Co. established in 1851. This firm has built up a large and prosperous trade in high-grade iron and steel, chiefly for railway work, both at home and abroad, and its products include 'Best Yorkshire' iron. The Monkbridge Co. was one of the earliest to install Siemens steel furnaces. Its present-day products are mainly railway wheels, axles and tyres. *Ref:2241.*

Hopperton

Situated on the York-Harrogate line, the station was opened by the East & West Yorkshire Railway on 30 October 1848; it was originally called Allerton, renaming occurred on 1 October 1925. Owing to the decline in rural stations in the 1950s, other lines in the area – Harrogate-Pateley Bridge and Knaresborough-Pilmoor – closed to passengers and, to make the service even less attractive, Hopperton saw its service much reduced; one weekday train each way to York and Harrogate – except Wednesday when there was an additional York service. Not unexpectedly there was a purge of wayside stations by the North Eastern Region, and closure to passengers occurred on 15 September 1958 with goods traffic ceasing on 5 November 1962. The line is still open with several intermediate stations remaining operational. Some work on, or around, the level crossing is taking place, as there are temporary traffic lights in operation; along with some displaced fencing. *Ref:2301.*

Hornsea Town

Above: The end is nigh at Hornsea Town on 16 April 1963, with platforms 1 and 2 decommissioned a two-car Class 105 unit stands in Platform 3. The Hull & Hornsea Railway opened the station on 28 March 1864; originally just Hornsea, the suffix Town was added on 25 September 1950 to avoid confusion with the Hornsey in north London. The line's original Hull terminus was at Wilmington, until 1 June 1864 when Paragon terminus was opened; the company was merged with the NER on 16 July 1866. The station closed to all traffic on 19 October 1964. The station building survives and is today a Grade II listed structure. *Ref:2231.*

Keighley

Opposite top: The first station, opened on 16 March 1847 by the Leeds & Bradford Extension Railway, was slightly to the north of the present site; with the rebuilt station opening on 6 May 1883, the station is located on the Airedale line 17 miles (27km) north-west of Leeds. The station was the junction for the MR's line to Oxenhope, opening on 15 April 1867. Keighley was also the terminus for the GNR (LNER) services to Halifax and Bradford. All traffic ceased from Keighley to Cullingworth in 1955 although rail access to the former GNR goods shed survived until 1961. The branch closed to passengers on 1 January 1962, with goods traffic ending on 18 June the same year. The branch was re-opened as a heritage railway, by the K&WVR Preservation Society, on 29 June 1968 and is now a popular tourist attraction. The train see here, headed by MR Class 3F No. 43586, was the K&WVRPS 'Worth Valley Special' rail tour that ran on Saturday 23 June 1962. *Ref:2574*

Kippax

Opposite bottom: The caption should probably read 'nice track, shame about the station'! The Permanent Way team, complete with look out, pose for the cameraman at Kippax during its freight only period. The station was on the western edge of the village adjacent to the hamlet of Great Preston. Like all the other stations on the Castleford-Garforth line, it had just one platform on the eastern side of the line, opening to passengers on 12 August 1878; it had however opened to goods traffic four months earlier. As with other sections of the line, the station did not possess a passing loop, though trains could pass in the freight loop that led into the goods yard. Unusually, in 1880, the station's water tower was used to supply fresh water to the people living in and around the station area; an outbreak of fever, diphtheria and diarrhoea in previous years had led to the railway company providing fresher water than that already available to the locals; it was not used to supply locomotives. The station had a goods shed to the south of the platform and the chief export was aggregate; a local quarry had a siding just to the north of the station. The stopping place was also the busiest station on the line as it served a larger and well-established village. In 1911, 44,000 tickets were issued compared to Ledston's 15,000. It closed to passengers on 22 January 1951, and then to goods on 30 September 1963. No trace of the station remains, though the track bed has been converted into a cycleway. *Ref:2347*

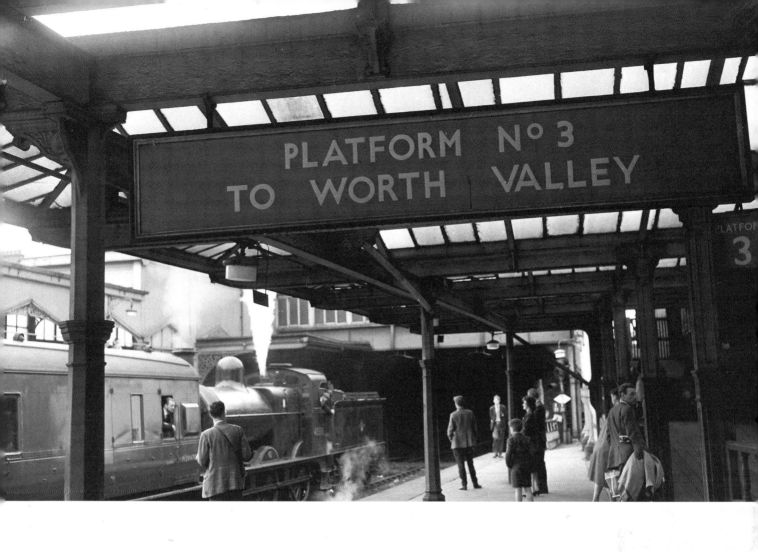

Leeds Central

The railways arrived in Leeds when the Leeds & Selby Railway (which became part of the NER) opened its line – its original terminus at Marsh Lane east of the city centre – opened on 22 September 1834. In 1840, the North Midland Railway (a constituent of the Midland Railway) constructed its line from Derby via Rotherham to a terminus at Hunslet Lane to the south, opening on 1 July 1840. It was soon extended to a more centrally located terminus on Wellington Street and was known as Wellington. Another station, Leeds Central (also on Wellington Street), was opened in 1854 by the Manchester & Leeds Railway and the LNWR; the railway station became owned jointly by the LNWR and the North Eastern Railway, but other companies had powers to run trains there, including the GNR and L&YR. On 1 April 1869, 'New' station opened as a joint enterprise by the LNWR and the North Eastern Railway. It connected the former Leeds & Selby Railway to the east with the LNWR lines to the west. A mile-long connection was built, carried entirely on viaducts and bridges. New station was built partially on a bridge over the River Aire, adjacent to Wellington station. The first rationalisation occurred in 1938, when two railway stations (New and Wellington) were combined to form Leeds City station, opening on 2 May that year. The north concourse and the Queens Hotel were built at this time. The third railway station, Leeds Central (the subject of these illustrations), was unaffected by these changes. Central closed on 1 May 1967, when its services were moved to Leeds City to consolidate all of Leeds' train services in one station. The last train left on 29 April 1967; this was a Saturday and as there was no Sunday service, the station closed with effect from the Monday. The last train was an early evening service to Harrogate operated by the usual Birmingham RC&W multiple unit. Detonators were placed on the track by railway staff that exploded as the train rolled away from the platform and past the signal box on its final departure. After closure, part of the station site became a Royal Mail sorting office, later partially redeveloped as the West Point residential development.

Above: The exterior of Leeds Central station. As can be seen the station was built above street level. The vehicle is a Ford Escort (produced between 1955 and 1961), based on the Squire (1955-1959); but with a lower trim level similar to the Anglia – a total of 33,131 were built. *Ref:1198.*

Opposite: The interior of the station looking along Platform 5, with railway staff going about the daily chores of checking the track and keeping the place tidy. On a sunny day the glass in the train shed roof casts a variety of shadows across the scene. *Ref:1172.*

Platform 3 is occupied by families, complete with luggage, awaiting their train as the annual holiday get away has started. The permanent way gang is maintaining the three-way point of the locomotive release roads of the terminal platforms. *Ref:1174.*

Leeds Wellington, not to be confused with Leeds Wellington Street, was opened as a temporary station by the Midland Railway on 1 July 1846, being replaced by the permanent version opening on 30th September 1850. A commuter strides purposefully along platform 4 at Wellington station. The carriage on the extreme right can be identified as No 20147, a Fowler-designed Non-Corridor Brake Third. *Ref:1302.*

Opposite top: Almost alongside the MR's Wellington terminus station, the LNWR and NER built their own station, opening on 1 April 1869 as Leeds New. A connection to the Leeds & Selby Railway's Marsh Lane line was opened on the same date. The 'City' name did not come into use until 2 May 1938 when the operation of both stations was combined as a cost-saving exercise. *Ref:1182.*

Opposite bottom: A queue at Leeds City, are they all bound for Whitby? Part of the route travelled would have been between Pickering and Grosmont closed by British Railways but it survives today as the heritage North Yorkshire Moors Railway. In summer steam services are extended to Whitby. At today's prices the cost of 12/6d (62½p) would seem a bargain. *Ref:1322.*

Above: As part of the project to rebuild City station to accommodate all Leeds services, a model was built so the public could see what the rebuilt station would look like. Most architect's models are to a 1/100th scale, useful for railway modellers as it enables Triang TT (Table Top) items to be used – note the DMU on the left of the image. *Ref:1186.*

Above: The old train shed at Leeds City in the throes of demolition. The contractors, Connell & Finnigan Ltd, was formed in 1953 and, working extensively with Manchester and Liverpool City Councils, demolished many air raid shelters after World War 2. The company then rapidly grew in the late 1950s and 1960s, mainly through the demolition of redundant gas works, railway stations, collieries, steel works, and numerous redundant warehouses in city centres across England. One wonders what the Yorkshire folk thought of a Manchester-based company demolishing their station! *Ref:1214.*

Opposite top: This is the concourse area constructed in 1938 to a design by W. H. Hamlyn – LMS chief architect – as part of the scheme to connect New and Wellington stations; Hamlyn was also responsible for the design of the Queens Hotel. After the station was rebuilt in the 1960s, the ex-Wellington terminal platforms were largely reduced to parcels use and the concourse deteriorated. Recent expansion has seen the Grade II listed concourse restored. It is unusually quiet; explained as the image was taken during a railway strike. Amongst the platform furniture, between the post box and vending machine, there is a 'special announcements' display board advertising excursions to Bridlington, Chesterfield, Derby, Birmingham, Nottingham and Liverpool. In addition Messrs. Heinz, Bass and Yardley are touting their goods through contemporary adverts. *Ref:1238.*

Opposite bottom: Leeds City The steel framework for the new parcels trolley gantry under construction. At the time of rebuilding, the carriage of parcels was still very much a profitable activity for BR. The first generation DMUs had the ability to haul parcels vans should the need arise. The final bays of the old train shed roof await demolition. This view is taken looking east and shows the ex-NER main line heading towards Neville Hill. *Ref:1254.*

Stations

Leeds City

It was business as usual during the reconstruction; a Metro-Cammell Class 101 stands in the platform. The British Railways House office block is under construction in the background. At this time a lot of the 'steam age' infrastructure was still visible including the water column. *Ref:1262.*

Manningham

Opposite: The station was the first stop out of Bradford on the Leeds & Bradford Railway, opened on 17 February 1868. Nearby was the locomotive depot; opening in 1872 as a single road building it was augmented in 1887 with a four-road shed. The latter was closed by the LMS around 1945, with the depot finally closing on 30 April 1967. Passenger services ceased on 22 March 1967, with freight traffic ending just over a year later. The Bradford Railway Circle used a hut on the platform for its meetings from the 1950s, until closure in 1965. Taken from the road bridge looking north towards Shipley, the image clearly shows the sighting board, that enables the train crew to see the signal indication against the sky. *Ref:2257*

Market Weighton

Above: The York & North Midland Railway was the first to reach the town, from York, with its terminus opening on 4 October 1847; the line from Selby opening on 1 August 1848. It remained a terminus for 18 years until the York line was extended to Beverley, opening on 1 May 1865. The Selby line was extended to Driffield on 2 April 1890 by the Scarborough, Bridlington & West Riding Junction Railway. By 1947 the overall roof was in need of repairs, but the LNER chose to replace it with steel awnings that survived until complete closure on 29 November 1965. *Ref:2471.*

Menston

Above: The original station here, Menston Junction, was opened on 1 March 1873, being replaced by the current one on 1 November 1875. Opened by the Midland Railway it was on their line from Apperley Junction to Burley-in-Wharfedale, from where trains could travel to either Ilkley or Otley via the Otley & Ilkley Joint Railway. The route to Otley was closed on 22 March 1965, but the Ilkley line (though also listed for closure in the 1963 Beeching Report) avoided a similar fate, being finally reprieved in 1972. Electric services at the station commenced in 1994. Nearby was the West Riding County Asylum, otherwise known as High Royds Hospital, opened in 1888 and closing in 2003, was for psychiatric patients. Standing to the west of the line it was served by a half-mile long private siding from just south of the station between 1883 and 1951. On the day of the photographer's visit Metro-Cammell (Class 101) and Derby lightweight (Class 108) DMUs are seen at the station. *Ref:2255.*

Morecambe Promenade

Opposite bottom: Built by the Midland Railway as the terminus of the former 'little' North Western Railway, Morecambe Promenade station first opened to passengersm on 24 March 1907. It served as a replacement for the inadequate Northumberland Street station (that was situated on the site of the current two platform Morecambe station). Promenade was built to cater for the summer influx of passengers with four main platforms and a goods siding. Upon opening there was some controversy over the segregation of passengers into 1st and 2nd class waiting rooms; generally passengers disapproved of this and chose to wait instead on the station concourse. The MR electrified the recently opened branch line from Heysham Harbour to Morecambe Promenade on 13 April 1908, with the main line to Lancaster soon afterwards. Three new three-car EMUs were purpose-built by the MR at Derby tooperate the service, which ran every 30 minutes throughout the day between the main LNWR station at Lancaster Castle and Heysham; maintenance facilities were provided at the station. Following Nationalisation in 1948 a number of significant changes occurred. In February 1951, after more than 40 years of service, the EMU sets were withdrawn and scrapped. These were replaced by steam-powered push-pull sets; however, in 1953 electric working was reinstated, still at 6,600V AC and using the same infrastructure, but this time at a 50Hz frequency (ultimately leading BR to adopt 25kV electrification). Three EMU sets built in 1914, and formerly used on the Willesden Junction-Earls Court service in London, were brought in to run the service, and a fourth set was added in 1957. In September 1958, the former LNWR terminus in the town, Euston Road, was closed to regular passenger traffic at the end of the summer timetable. Promenade survived the Beeching axe, but by the late 1980s tourism in Morecambe was rapidly declining. Traffic levels were significantly lower than they had been at their peak 30 years before. The four platform, fully signalled, layout had remained largely unaltered and was now far too large for the modest service (1-2 trains per hour) then in operation. In 1993 the decision was taken to close Promenade and replace it with a new station situated slightly further inland and closer to the town centre. A final commemorative rail tour visited the station the evening before its official closure on 7 February 1994. This view is along the platform towards the buffer stops. The extensive track layout shows that the town was once a popular destination. *Ref:1837.*

Normanton

Above: The original station was opened by the North Midland Railway (NMR), on 30 June 1840, on its main line towards Leeds, creating an interchange station between the NMR, the York & North Midland Railway and the Manchester & Leeds Railway – establishing a three company junction. Construction began in 1837 under the supervision of George Stephenson for the North Midland. Followed by an addition from the York & Midland Railway and finally by the Manchester & Leeds line. This gave Normanton access across much of the country. The NMR, already open between Derby and Rotherham (Masborough), was opened between Rotherham and Leeds (Hunslet Lane) on 1 July 1840, as was the Y&NMR between Normanton (on the NMR) and Burton Salmon (the line between Burton Salmon and York already being open). The M&LR route between Normanton and Hebden Bridge followed, opening on 5 October 1840; on 1 March 1841, the final section of the M&LR route to Manchester was opened. The Leeds and Manchester lines crossed a 51 mile (82km) stretch across the Pennines and at the time boasted the world's longest railway station platform at Normanton – a quarter of a mile (400m) long. The station closed to public goods traffic on 30 September 1953; with the station losing many of its services in the aftermath of the Beeching Report, with both express and local trains on the NMR main line ceasing to call in 1968 and trains to York ending in 1970, leaving only Hallam line trains to serve the station. Doing a very good job of looking derelict, this is the south end of the station with an unidentified tank locomotive shunting a short rake of wagons. Poking over the top of the hill is the headgear of St Johns Colliery. William Locke and John Warrington of Newland Hall, Normanton, opened the colliery in 1870. It passed into the hands of the National Coal Board in 1947 and worked until closure in 1973. *Ref:1825.*

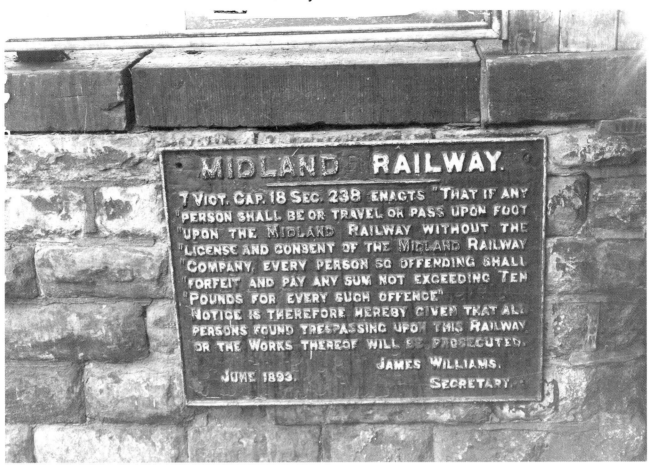

Stations

Opposite top: Virtually all railway companies used a copious quantity of signs, advising people not to trespass. This example was photographed at Normanton. *Ref:1829.*

Opposite bottom: Brush Type 4 No. 1603 runs a passenger service through the extensive station. The NMR was closed completely in 1988 south of the former Goose Hill junction (where it diverged from the M&L line to Wakefield) although part of the route further south remains open to serve a glassworks at Monk Bretton, near Barnsley. This has led to much of the railway infrastructure here becoming redundant and being removed – the main buildings have been demolished, the sidings and goods lines lifted, the bay platforms filled in and the main island shortened considerably. The old Station Hotel still stands, but it has been converted into residential apartments. No 1603 entered service in July 1964; renumbered as 47475 in April 1974, it was withdrawn in July 1999. *Ref:1831.*

Queensbury

Below: The station was unusual due to its triangular shape, and at its opening the only other example of this arrangement was Ambergate in Derbyshire; since then Shipley station, also in West Yorkshire, has gained platforms on all three sides. Of the stations on the Queensbury lines, this was the most ambitious. The station was located some distance away from the town itself, and at a considerably lower altitude. Queensbury is one of the highest settlements in England and the station was built at around 400ft (120m) lower than the village; access being via a poorly lit footpath. There were also three signal boxes at the station, one for each junction on the three station approaches – from Bradford, Keighley and Halifax. The station was opened to traffic on 12 July 1879, closing to passengers on 23 May 1955; final closure for general goods came on 11 September 1963. Almost the entire station infrastructure has now been demolished. The station site is one of the trailheads on The Great Northern Railway Trail that forms a path to Cullingworth along the former track bed. *Ref:1522.*

Skipton

The original station was opened on 7 September 1847 by the Leeds & Bradford Extension Railway, as a temporary terminus of its line from Bradford. The line was extended to Colne a year later on 2 October 1848. The following year, the 'little' North Western Railway opened a line from Skipton to Ingleton on 30 July 1849 (which was extended to Lancaster and Morecambe in 1850). On 30 April 1876, Skipton station was relocated a quarter of a mile north-west of its original location; by now, the Midland Railway had absorbed both the Leeds & Bradford and North Western Railways. The new station coincided with the opening of the Midland's Settle-Carlisle line, which made Skipton a station on the London St Pancras to Glasgow main line. The new station had four platforms and cost over £15,000, compared with the original station's cost of £2,300. Two platforms were added to serve the Skipton to Ilkley line, which opened on 1 October 1888. These platforms were at a slightly higher level on a rising gradient, as the new line ran south-west of the existing line and then crossed over it by bridge eastwards. The Yorkshire Dales Railway, a short branch to Grassington from 1902 to 1930, also used these platforms at a later date. Passenger services to Ilkley ceased on 22 March 1965, after which their platforms were closed to passengers and the access subway was bricked off. However, the line through what was platform 5 is still in use as a single-track freight line to Swinden Quarry via the former Yorkshire Dales line. The track through platform 6 has been lifted. Today the station has four platforms serving Leeds, Bradford, Carlisle, Lancaster and Morecambe.

Above: Built at Derby in November 1954, this is a view of a two-car Lightweight unit, No. 79008 leading, arriving at Skipton. What became know as 'First Generation' units had the ability to haul tail loads, enabling additional passenger accommodation as seen here – or even vans – to be added. The aluminium-bodied units did not fare too well, lasting less than 15 years in traffic, with a number withdrawn due to accident damage. *Ref:1570.*

Stanningley

Opposite top: The station, also called Stanningley for Farsley, opened on 1 August 1854 as a stop on the Leeds, Bradford & Halifax Junction Railway, later part of the GNR, from Leeds Central station to Bradford Adolphus Street. On 1 April 1878 a branch from Stanningley to Pudsey Greenside was opened that eventually evolved into the Pudsey loop line. Having been renamed Stanningley for Farsley, the name reverted to Stanningley on 12 June 1961. The station closed on 1 January 1968, while the line itself has remained open, with trains on the Calder Valley line passing the site of the former station and calling at New Pudsey about a mile to the west, which opened on 1 May 1967. The station had a sizeable goods yard; the goods shed has survived almost intact and is used by a builders' merchant, while the station building is used as business premises. *Ref:1476.*

Wetherby

Opposite bottom: This view is of the second station at Wetherby, built by the North Eastern Railway. Opened on 1 July 1902 it was on the line connecting Leeds (Crossgates) to the Church Fenton-Harrogate line. It replaced an earlier station on the Church Fenton-Harrogate line, the latter remaining open as a goods station. By the 1950s private car ownership would start signalling the demise of the line and closure to passenger traffic occurred on 6 January 1964. Freight traffic struggled on until 4 April 1966 as the station was not close enough to the racecourse to make the carriage of horses viable. Incidentally, BR ceased the carriage of livestock in 1972. Up until 1963, Racecourse Specials ran to Wetherby railway station from Bradford Interchange on race days. As the first station, on York Road, had closed many years before, on 1 July 1902, the only rail access was via the station on Linton Road at the other end of Wetherby from the racecourse. Sandwiched between two over-bridges, the station would make a neat model railway. *Ref:1839.*

Stations

Wilsden

Opposite: The Great Northern Railway built Wilsden station on the Queensbury-Keighley line. A number of the stations on the Queensbury triangle routes had extensive goods yards as many of the settlements served had mills and factories that provided traffic until the arrival of the road haulage industry. It was sited some two miles from the village it was named after, being closer to the small hamlet of Harecroft. It was opened on 1 July 1886, being the last station to open on the Queensbury-Keighley section of the line. Closure to passengers came on 23 May 1955, with goods traffic ceasing on 11 November 1963. The traffic was sparse, as can be seen here as an unidentified LNER Class N1 0-6-2T departs. *Ref:2454.*

Withernsea

Bottom: Opened on 27 June 1854, the station was the terminus of the Hull & Holderness Railway that ran from Hull to the coast at Withernsea. Initially independent, the company was too small to survive and was leased to the NER from 1 January 1860, outright purchase coming a couple of years later. Trains ran into Hull's Paragon Street station, via the Victoria Docks branch, from 1 June 1864. DMUs were introduced at the beginning of 1957, with further cost-cutting proposals suggested; it was all to no avail, the line was closed to passengers under the Beeching Report on 19 October 1964. Goods traffic survived until the following May. Having arrived at their destination aboard a Cravens Class 105 DMU, the passengers make their way out of the station on 16 April 1963. *Ref:2251.*

York to Pickering: Coxwold

The photographer appears to have travelled on a freight train in July 1964, just prior to the cessation of goods services over the line. The stations at Coxwold and Gilling were opened on 19 May 1853 by the York, Newcastle & Berwick Railway (YN&BR); the railway was formed in 1847 by the amalgamation of the York & Newcastle Railway and the Newcastle & Berwick Railway. Helmsley was a later addition to the network, opening on 9 October 1871 by the North Eastern Railway. Regular passenger services to Malton ceased between Thirsk and Pickering on 2 February 1953; however, occasional special passenger trains continued to use the station until 27 July 1964. Freight traffic continued until 10 August 1964.

Above: Coxwold station with the signalman looking as if he is about to throw the single line token to the driver. Note the raised coal drop siding on the left, enabling fuel to be delivered to the local merchant in hopper wagons. The locomotive is carrying a 50A shed plate on the cab, which was the code for York depot. *Ref:1791.*

Gilling

Opposite top: The station for passengers wishing to go to Ampleforth College and special trains would be run at the start and the end of term time. The college was equidistant between Ampleforth and Gilling stations, but access was easier from Gilling. On 30 August 1895 the college signed an agreement with the NER to build a tramway from Gilling station. Construction of the 3ft (0.91m) gauge Decauville track tramway started in 1894 (a year before the agreement was signed) and it was opened by Christmas 1895 to connect Gilling with the College and its gasworks. The tramway was built by Mr White at a cost of £1,072 8s 7d (equivalent to £120,000 in 2019). Staff and pupils were transported to the college from the station, but they were secondary to the main traffic that was coal for the gas boilers. Alexander Penney & Sons, engineers of London, provided six tip wagons. The line was horse-drawn throughout its history, closing in 1923 when the college went over to electric lighting with the gas works closing.

BR Class 03 204hp diesel shunter No. D2111 was constructed at Doncaster in November 1960, surviving in traffic until withdrawal in July 1980. *Ref:1789.*

Helmsley

Opposite bottom: This was the largest station in Ryedale, handling most of the traffic although it was beaten by Kirbymoorside for passenger traffic. Most of the town, and surrounding countryside, was owned by the Earl of Feversham who required certain conditions to be met by the NER before giving permission to build the line and station. As a result the station was more lavish than others on the line with first and second class waiting rooms amongst other refinements. It remained gas lit throughout its life. To ensure the NER continued to comply with the Earl's wishes he was given a seat on the NER Board. The line from Gilling to Helmsley opened on 9 October 1871. The extension to Kirbymoorside opened on 1 January 1874. No. D2111 and crew are preparing to depart. The shunter is holding his 'badge of office', the shunting pole used for uncoupling wagons, to save going between them. *Ref:1787.*

Pockley Gates

Opposite: The services of permanent crossing keeper have been dispensed with, as a member of the train crew closes the crossing gates behind the train. Although the location is not given it may well be Pockley Gates, between Helmsley and Nawton stations, on the return journey. *Ref:1785.*

Kirbymoorside

This page: Kirbymoorside railway station served the market town of Kirkbymoorside (note the different spelling), opening on 1 January 1878. It was built by the North Eastern Railway as Kirby Moorside; being renamed as Kirbymoorside on 31 May 1948. As with a lot of stations it did not survive the 1953 cull, closing to regular passenger traffic on 2 February – along with the track east to Pickering. The line still saw excursion traffic and a poster for a Ramblers' Association special for 3 May 1964 shows the destination as Kirkby Moorside; the cost of the return trip from Bradford was 18 shillings and six pence (92.5p). All services finally ceased on 10 August 1964. The train is arriving at Kirbymoorside, and the photographer is looking back along the track as No. D2111 and its short freight arrive at what is now the end of the line. *Ref:1783.*

Chapter 2

Steam at Work

Blea Moor Tunnel

Opposite: Situated on the Settle-Carlisle line between Ribblehead Viaduct and Dent station, the tunnel is 2,629yd (2,413m) in length. Built by the Midland Railway, construction commenced in 1872 taking over four years to complete at a cost of £109,000 (over £10m in today's prices). Some 500ft below the surface of the moor it was named after; it required seven shafts to be sunk from the moor above with 16 teams of workers. Following completion four were filled in, with three being retained for ventilation. No. 44324, built at St Rollox works in January 1928, continued in service until November 1961. *Ref:1462*.

Kildwick

Above: LMS 'Royal Scot' No. 46113 *Cameronian* is at the head of the 'Thames-Clyde Express' on 24 September 1951. Commencing in September 1927, the train ran over the Midland main line, the Settle & Carlisle and the Glasgow & South Western lines on its journey from London St Pancras to Glasgow St Enoch (later Glasgow Central). No. 46113 was built by the North British Locomotive Co in September 1927 – it was one of 50 built that year as the LMS was short of front line motive power. It was rebuilt, as was the rest of the class, with a larger boiler, new cylinders and double chimney, and withdrawal came in December 1962. *Ref:2413*.

Kirkstall

Opposite top: Fowler Class 4P No. 41196 and train are seen at Kirkstall on 24 October 1951. These locomotives were based on the Midland Railway 'compounds' – a system involving one high and two low-pressure cylinders to improve efficiency. Adopted as a standard design by the LMS, 190 locomotives were constructed between 1924 and 1932. Vulcan Foundry built No. 1196 in March 1927, it being withdrawn in July 1958. Despite carrying its BR number, 41196, since July 1948, the locomotive still has LMS emblazoned on its tender. *Ref:1718.*

Knottingley

Opposite bottom: At the head of a Manchester-Hull express at Knottingley on 23 August 1951 is Stanier Class 4MT 2-6-4T No. 42477. Entering traffic in 1935 this class was a development of Fowler's locomotives that, via Stanier and Fairburn, ultimately led to the design of the BR Standard Class 4MT 2-6-4Ts. No. 42477 was built at Derby in January 1937, it was allocated to Goole (25C) from September 1950 to March 1956; the locomotive was in service until July 1965. *Ref:1528.*

Leeds Central

Above: With King George V celebrating 25 years on the Throne in 1935 the LNER's Board of Directors decided to commemorate the event with a new named train. From receipt of the order and the start of the drawings on 28 March 1935, both locomotive and carriages were completed 25 weeks later. The initial locomotive, No. 2509 *Silver Link,* ran a trial trip on 27 September 1935 reaching a speed of 112½mph (181km/h), and averaged 100mph (160km/h) for 43 miles – the locomotive was three weeks old and barely run in at the time. No. 2509 and its seven-coach train formed the first of the LNER's streamlined services, the 'Silver Jubilee' the first of three 'streamlined trains' – the third was the 'West Riding Ltd', seen here at Leeds Central behind No. 4495 *Golden Fleece.* The engine *was* originally named *Great Snipe* when it entered service in August 1937; being renamed and repainted from LNER green to blue with added stainless steel embellishments prior to commencement of the service on 27 September 1937. Unlike the 'Silver Jubilee' service, the 'West Riding Ltd' did resume after World War 2. *Ref:1176.*

Leeds City (Wellington)

Top: A pair of LMS 'Jubilees' are seen here, No. 5552 *Silver Jubilee* was built in December 1934. However, not all is what it seems, as in 1935 No. 5642 (built at Crewe, June 1934) exchanged numbers with the original 5552 and was finished in black enamel paint with cast chromium plated letters and numerals along with chromium plated dome and boiler bands. It was named to celebrate the silver jubilee of King eorge V, giving the name to the class. Judging by the presence of station staff and a police officer, something special is happening. *Ref:1300.*

Bottom: Although carrying the 'Waverley' headboard, No. 45697 *Achilles* (built Crewe in April 1936), is actually at the head of a rail tour organised by the Warwickshire Railway Society on 11 December 1965. Running from Birmingham New Street to Edinburgh Waverley the locomotive was at the head of the train for the Leeds City-Skipton-Waverley section. Note the cab carries a yellow stripe, this indicated that it should not be used south of Crewe following completion of overhead electrification from London. *Ref:1314.*

The LMS ran the 'Thames-Clyde Express' between London St Pancras and Glasgow St Enoch over the Midland Main Line, Settle & Carlisle and Glasgow & South Western from September 1927. The service was accelerated in the early 1930s using more powerful locomotives in the shape of the 'Jubilees'. No 45739 *Ulster* (built December 1936 at Crewe) is seen here on 9 August 1951. It has attracted quite a few young enthusiasts, some no doubt underlining the details in their contemporary Ian Allan spotters guides. A similar service ran between London St Pancras and Edinburgh Waverley, originally known as the Thames-Forth Express it was renamed 'The Waverley' by BR in 1957. *Ref:1275*

William Stanier's Class 5MT 4-6-0s were a fairly standard machine until H G Ivatt took over as Chief Mechanical Engineer in 1945. No. 44754 was built at Crewe Works in April 1948. It was one of a batch of 10 locomotives fitted with Caprotti valve gear, in place of the usual Walschaerts arrangement. The low running plates gave them a distinctive appearance. No. 44754 carries the early British Railways tender lettering whilst the leading coach retains LMS livery. *Ref:1610.*

Above: Following Sir Nigel Gresley's death in service on 5 April 1941, he was replaced by Edward Thompson as Chief Mechanical Engineer. Following Thompson's retirement in 1946, Arthur Peppercorn took over as the last CME of the LNER. The final 15 Pacifics to Thompson's design were reworked by Peppercorn and Class A2 No. 525 *A. H. Peppercorn* was the last LNER locomotive to enter traffic before Nationalisation. No. 525 leaves Leeds Central on 22 March 1948. *Ref:1286.*

Liverpool

Opposite: Liverpool Lime Street is the main station serving the city; opened in August 1836, it is the oldest terminus main line station still in use in the world. A branch off the West Coast main line from London Euston terminates at the station, as does the original Liverpool & Manchester Railway. Having quickly realised that their existing Crown Street station was too far away from the city centre, the L&MR commenced construction of the more central Lime Street station in October 1833. It was officially opened on 15 August 1836; proving to be so popular within six years of its opening, that expansion had become necessary. The first was completed during 1849 at a total cost of £15,000 (equivalent to £1.57m in 2019). During 1867, work upon a further expansion of the station commenced, during which the present northern arched train shed was built. Upon completion, the train shed was the largest such structure in the world, featuring a span of 200ft (61m), as well as the first to make extensive use of iron. In 1879, a second parallel southern train shed was completed. Following nationalisation, in 1948, Lime Street Station was the subject of various upgrades and alterations. In 1962, regular electric services between Lime Street and Crewe were started and, in 1966, the station hosted the launch of the first InterCity service, which saw the introduction of a regular 100mph (160km/h) service between Liverpool and London. During the 1970s, a new urban rail network, known as Merseyrail, was developed, while all other long-distance terminal stations in Liverpool were closed, all services being centralised at Lime Street. 'Rebuilt Royal Scot' class No. 46126 *Royal Army Service Corps* is seen here leaving Liverpool Lime Street with what is claimed to be the Royal Train. However, the locomotive is displaying the head code for an express passenger service. No. 46126 was built in 1927 by the North British Locomotive Co in Glasgow. It was rebuilt with a Stanier-designed boiler in June 1945, and withdrawn in September 1963. *Ref:1688.*

Neville Hill

Two light locomotives run towards the cameraman in the shape of Class D49 No. 62748 *The Southwold* and 'B1' 4-6-0 No. 61274. The first 25 Class D49s were named after Shire counties, with the remaining 50 named after Hunts, No. 62748 being one of the latter. Running away from the camera is an unidentified 'WD' class 2-8-0, the formation of the first few wagons seems to imply that the load might be of flammable material as the leading mineral wagon appears to be empty. *Ref:2191.*

Early LNER Pacifics

At the time of the Grouping in 1923 the NER was the largest and most prosperous of the railway companies that would make up the LNER, providing the general manager of the new company. However the chief mechanical engineer of the NER, Sir Vincent Raven, was at retirement age and the new post was eventually offered to Nigel Gresley of the GNR. Gresley had introduced his 'A1' class Pacific in April 1922, and Raven was anxious to show that the NER could keep up with the race for increased power. Raven's Pacific design was authorised at the same time as the introduction of the 'A1' class, publicised in the railway press in July 1922, although the first two examples did not appear from Darlington Works until late December, and only one of them ran before the formation of the LNER. Raven's new class was an enlarged version of the 'Z' class Atlantics with a larger boiler, larger cylinders and wide firebox. They shared with the later Gresley 'K3' class the record for the largest diameter boiler in Britain, at 6ft. Because of the great length of their parallel boilers, the locomotives earned the nickname 'Skittle-alleys'. Comparative trials between the first examples of the Gresley 'A1' and Raven 'A2' classes conducted in the summer of 1923 showed that the 'A1' was a more technically advanced machine and no more 'A2s' were built; the NER adopting the Gresley design as its standard express passenger locomotive.

On this page, examples of the rival designs are seen arriving at York over the almost 90 degree crossover at the station.
Top: Raven's LNER Class 'A2' No. 2402 *City of York* entered traffic in March 1924. Originally allocated to Gateshead, the class spent their first 10 years running between Grantham and Edinburgh. No. 2402 also had the melancholy distinction of being the the first LNER-built locomotive to be scrapped in July 1936. *Ref:1536.*

Bottom: The winning design – Gresley's 'A1' class – in virtually the same position on the crossing clearly shows the design differences. Built at Doncaster in November 1924, it was rebuilt as an 'A3' in September 1943 and after an operational life of 39 years was withdrawn in May 1963. No. 2552 *Sansovino* was named after a British racehorse that ran twelve times with six wins. As part of a general LNER post World War 2 renumbering scheme, the locomotive was renumbered 53 – becoming BR No. 60053. *Sansovino* was withdrawn on 27 May 1963 and scrapped at Doncaster a matter of days later. *Ref:1682.*

Wortley Sidings

Above: The Leeds & Bradford and Leeds & Thirsk lines met at Armley junction, just to the north west of Leeds city centre; Canal Street is to the left of the tracks with Hattersley's Spindle Works hiding behind the signal box. What looks like a church spire is part of the facade of the Albion Works building constructed in 1859 by Greenwood & Batley. The company could manufacture almost any product from war munitions – a 14in (35.56cm) torpedo was exhibited in 1891 – to tramcars. Well known amongst railway enthusiasts the company built 1,367 electric locomotives, with many exported around the world. In April 1980 the receivers were called in and G&B became part of the Hunslet Group who continued to use the name 'Greenbat' for its range of battery locomotives. The left line leading off the bottom of the illustration was to the New Wortley Gas Works that was acquired in 1869 by Leeds Corporation along with two other gas companies located in the City. The LMS Class 4F 0-6-0s were a development of the Midland Railway's similar locomotives. No. 4108 was built at Crewe Works in January 1925, surviving in traffic until December 1959. The load of two bridge girders are at the maximum height the loading gauge will permit and have been loaded on to specially designed bogies, with open mineral wagons placed as 'runners' helping to spread the weight. The driver looks towards the camera as if the event was planned. *Ref:1236.*

V2 at York

Opposite: The Gresley lineage can clearly be seen in his 'V2' class 2-6-2 design as No. 917 departs from York. In effect the class was a shortened Pacific with a pony truck replacing the leading bogie; rapidly demonstrated an ability to run fast with heavy loads, on passenger trains as well as express goods. The initial locomotive, No. 4771 *Green Arrow*, carried the name of a fast freight service instigated by the LNER in 1936. A total of 184 'V2s', in 11 batches, were constructed between 1936 and 1944. Built at Darlington in August 1940 as No. 4888, and renumbered 917 in December 1946, it was withdrawn on 13 April 1962. As BR No. 60917 the locomotive was loaned to the Southern Region in 1953 whilst the home grown Bulleid Pacifics were being checked for axle flaws. *Ref:1434.*

Chapter 3
Civil Engineering

Arthington Viaduct

The Viaduct, also known as Castley Viaduct and listed as the Wharfedale Viaduct, carries the Harrogate line across the Wharfe Valley between Arthington and Castley. Built by the Leeds & Thirsk Railway the viaduct was constructed between 1845 and 1849. It is on a curve of some 500yds (457m) in length, with 21 semi-circular arches. Henry Cooper Marshall, Chairman of the Leeds & Thirsk Railway, laid the foundation stone on 31 March 1846; the line opened on 10 July 1849 when the nearby Bramhope Tunnel, another key component of the route, was completed. In excess of 50,000 tons of stone were used in its construction. It is now a Grade II listed structure. *Ref:1470.*

Woodhead Tunnels

The first tunnel, a single line bore at Woodhead, was constructed by the Sheffield, Ashton-under-Lyne & Manchester Railway. Work commenced in 1837, being designed by the railway engineer Charles Vignoles, who was later substituted by the civil engineer Joseph Locke. When opened in 1845,

Woodhead was one of the world's longest railway tunnels and the first under the Pennines. The second tunnel, also a single line bore, was completed in 1853. With both tunnels subject to heavy traffic; they were difficult to maintain because of their narrowness, with traffic estimated to be around 250 trains per day in both directions. As the size of both tunnels was too restricted to allow for electrification, it was decided to construct a third tunnel in the 1950s. This tunnel opened in June 1953, almost 100 years after the second, with the transport minister, Alan Lennox-Boyd, performing the opening ceremony. It had cost £4.3 million (almost £2m over budget) and tragically six people lost their lives during the work. The gathering is seen here on opening day with 1,500Vdc locomotive No. 26020 doing the honours. Traffic on the route diminished, and in 1970, the last passenger services ran through the tunnel; the last freight train passed through in 1981 after which it was closed. Various proposals have been made to reopen the route, but doing so would probably mean another tunnel under the Pennines. The opening event must have given the locomotive some fans, as it is now the sole survivor of its class and part of the National Collection. *Ref:2349 (left) 1456 (above).*

Ingrow East Signal box

Left: Ingrow East is situated to the east of the present K&WVR station. Opened by the Great Northern Railway on 7 April 1884, it was on the extension of the original Bradford to Thornton line, via Queensbury, that had opened earlier. Just north of the station the line joined the Midland's Keighley-Oxenhope route. Originally called Ingrow, the East was added by BR on 2 March 1951. Closure to passenger traffic occurred on 23 May 1955, with freight traffic surviving until complete closure on 28 June 1965. The small 'room' to the left of the landing was the toilet, the signalman not being able to leave his post to walk to the facilities in the adjacent station building. *Ref:2582.*

Tollerton Signal box

Above: In January 1961 a new box was opened 300yd south-east of Tollerton station on the upside of the tracks beside the entrance to the station's sidings. The box was part of the upgrade of the East Coast main line following completion of the 1959 project to quadruple the line. It controlled 12 route miles until replaced by a new facility at York that controlled a longer stretch of the main line in May 1989. An unidentified 'WD' 2-8-0 heads past the box with a freight train in tow. *Ref:1442.*

Weed killing train

Opposite left: A regular task was the need to travel the network and dose the track with copious quantities of weed killer. A source of water was required; this being carried in either redundant locomotive tenders or tank wagons. Regular top ups would have been required, a lot easier when steam was in regular use. With the supply piped to the coach a means of pumping it was required and the mechanical drive for the pump gear is illustrated. *Ref:2311.*

Opposite right: The business end of the 'spraying' coach. The end windows would have been added to enable the operators to see where to spray; generally the train would have been propelled, as a good view of the track ahead was required. No waiting passengers would have wanted to be covered in what was then a potent weed killer. The system is still in use on Network Rail as a means of controlling weed growth. *Ref:2456.*

Doncaster South Signal Box

Opposite bottom: The current station was opened in September 1850 by the GNR, replacing a temporary structure constructed a year earlier. It was rebuilt in its present form in 1938 and has had several slight modifications since that date, most notably in 2006, with new booking office for tickets and information, three new lifts, refurbished staircases and subway. The station Booking Hall and Offices were Grade II listed in April 1988. Doncaster North and South signal boxes were part of a new power-signalling scheme being planned for Doncaster by the LNER before World War 2. Some work had started but it was not until 1949, then under British Railways, before both these boxes were in use. The original South Box was situated at the end of the station. *Ref:1640.*

This page, top: The interior of the original South Box on 5 January 1949. The signalman does not look too impressed with the presence of the photographer; generally signalmen were solitary characters, and did not appreciate 'official' visitors. 'Officialdom' was probably discussing the box's demise, though judging by the state of the interior it was probably not before time. *Ref:1642*

This page, bottom: Inside the new South Box, all three images carry the same date, so the change over was taking place. Both North and South Signal Boxes, along with the old colour light signals, were replaced when overhead electrification came and a new Power Box was built, opening in July 1979. In 2020 most of the signalling will be transferred to York Rail Operating Centre, with full closure planned for 2025. *Ref:1638.*

Bradford

Above: The railways were always keen to find alternative income streams, at some stage it was realised that the railways had ready-made poster-boards. The bridge seen here at Greengates, Bradford, carries advertising for the Thornton Engineering Co, of 150 Manningham Lane; a motor dealership that sold the products of the Rootes Group. The bridge was on the GNR's Shipley branch that lost its passenger services in 1931; freight traffic lasted longer with the Cutlers Junction-Idle section closing on 2 November 1964; the Idle-Shipley section on 7 October 1968. The Cutlers Junction-Laisterdyke section, which served an English Electric factory at Thornbury, survived until the early 1980s. In 1905 Thornton Engineering had produced the 'Teco' automobile, and in 1907/8 manufactured the 'Celtic' car; and advertised itself as 'The Motor Car Depot of the North'. The brand names depicted here all now consigned to history. *Ref:1474.*

Opposite: Located just to the south of Bradford Exchange station was St Dunstans, this was where the L&YR's line running southwards crossed the GNR's Leeds-Bradford-Halifax line. The railway's steam crane has been brought in by a 'WD' 2-8-0, standing to the north of the bridge, with a second on the south side. The new girders carry the manufacturer's name - Samuel Butler & Co of Stanningley. The image was taken from the Ripley Street overbridge that crossed both lines. The GNR's St Dunstans station closed in 1952 – three years before passenger services were withdrawn from the Queensbury triangle routes – can be seen in the haze behind the crane; the carriages are occupying the L&YR's carriage sidings. As well as structural steelwork Samuel Butler & Co supplied steam cranes – the majority of which were supplied to the 'colonies'. *Ref:1947.*

Snow, the winter of 1947

Beginning on 23 January 1947, the UK experienced several cold spells that brought large drifts of snow to the country, blocking roads and railways, which caused problems transporting coal to the power stations. Many had to shut down, forcing severe restrictions to cut power consumption, including restricting domestic electricity to 19 hours per day and cutting some industrial supplies completely. In addition, radio broadcasts were limited, television services were suspended, some magazines were ordered to stop publishing, and newspapers were reduced in content. Towards the end of February, there were also fears of a food shortage as supplies were cut off and vegetables were frozen into the ground. A little over 10 years later events were to repeat themselves as early 1958 saw further disruptions to services due to the severe winter as the image at Driffield shows. Five years later the winter of 1963 saw a repeat of events – once again severe weather resulted in shortages and service interruptions.

Above: One of the problems faced was the snow and ice compacting between the rails. Although it is not clear in the photograph, Class J27 No. 65827 and 'A8' No. 69835 have come to grief between Driffield and Malton at the end of February 1958, whilst hauling a mix of three general utility vans and box vans. Although no passengers would be inconvenienced, the train was probably carrying urgently needed foodstuffs. *Ref:2383.*

Opposite: Photographed from the Barnsley direction, the yard to the west of Penistone is seen under snow in February 1947. The line off to the left went to Sheffield. The northern end of the junction led to Penistone station where a further split took place, with lines to Huddersfield and Manchester (via Woodhead Tunnel). At the time of the photograph there is no sign of the forthcoming electrification. *Ref:205.*

Chapter 4

Accidents

Ardsley

Opposite: Built by the LNER at Doncaster Works as a Class A3, No. 2743 entered traffic on 22 August 1928. It was renumbered 89 under the company's 1946 renumbering system and became 60089 on Nationalisation of the railways in 1948. The 'A3s' generally carried names of the winners of major horse races, with the name Felstead taken from the winner of the 1928 Derby. No. 60089 was involved in an accident at Ardsley – with a stationary 'V2' – whilst working a King's Cross-Leeds express on 26 October 1959, this before returning to Scotland, having been recently overhauled. The locomotive and first two carriages were derailed; fortunately there were no fatalities. Despite the severity of the damage the Scottish Region wanted its locomotive back. With class mate, No. 60104 Solario, being in the works 'on decision' at this time – November 1959 – it was agreed to withdraw No. 60104 and use it as a parts-donor to enable No. 60089 to return to traffic. Withdrawal for No. 60089 finally came in October 1963. The top image (left) shows the damaged front end and above the engine being re-railed using hydraulic jacks. *Ref:1006 (top), 1648 (bottom).*

Hest Bank

Above: Hest Bank the morning after the 10.10pm Glasgow Central-London (Kensington Olympia) sleeper service was derailed by a broken rail, on 29 May 1965. The rear nine coaches were derailed with the train splitting into three sections. The diesel and first three carriages remained on the rails – the second portion of four vehicles, including three sleepers, came to rest between the platforms – the final portion of four sleeping carriages and brake van ended up on the low embankment on their sides. Injuries were slight with no fatalities. The two steam locomotives in the view were not involved with the accident but have brought the steam cranes and breakdown crews to the scene. If this accident happened today the adjacent road would be crowded with sightseers, the few non-railway personnel visible are just going about their business as usual! The station closed to passengers on 3 February 1969 and was subsequently demolished along with removal of the five Camping Coaches. This is the only location on the West Coast main line where the coast line and Irish Sea can be seen from the railway. *Ref:2044.*

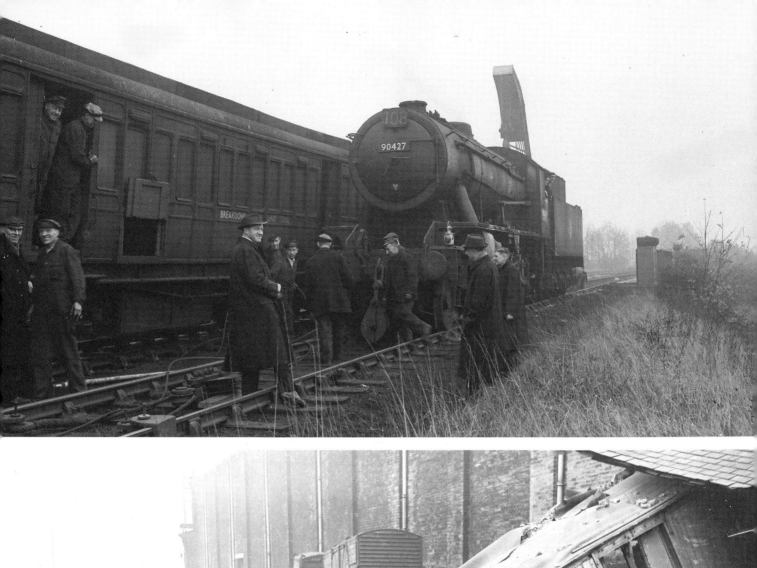

Opposite top: This incident is recorded as being in the Hull area with the Breakdown Train called to a derailment, although the crane is also in attendance. The image is of interest as it shows part of the pulling tackle arrangement; note the rail clamp and pulleys attached to the track, of more interest is the block and pulley attached to the locomotive's drawbar. With the locomotive crew enjoying their 'day out' with the breakdown crew, the locomotive is War Department Class 8F 2-8-0 No. 90427, built by the Vulcan Foundry in October 1943; it was initially numbered 77112 and purchased by the LNER on 16 March 1947. Then numbered 3106, it became No. 63106 upon Nationalisation, before being renumbered in the BR Standard locomotive number series as 90427 on 23 December 1950. It was withdrawn in June 1967. The coach – DE320139, Breakdown Train Unit (Tool) – was built by the Great Central Railway in 1905 as a Third class compartment carriage. Being converted for use by the breakdown train crews in November 1952. According to the shed plate the locomotive was allocated to 50B, Hull Dairycoates, between December 1958 and November 1963, dating the incident to this time frame. *Ref:1817.*

Bradford, Adolphus Street

At one time Bradford had three terminus stations, operated by three different companies. Kirkgate (later Forster Square) was operated by the Leeds & Bradford; Exchange, operated by the L&YR; and Adolphus Street, operated by the Leeds, Bradford & Halifax Junction Railway. The latter was closed to passengers on 7January 1867, remaining open as a goods depot until closing completely on 1 May 1972, although it appears traffic may have ended well before that date. A major accident occurred on 10 November 1964. At Bradford Ivatt Class 4MT No. 43072 was working a 21 vehicle empty wagon train from Ardsley. The driver lost control and ran into the yard at around 50mph (80km/h), the crew jumped clear before the train demolished the buffer stops and dropped 30ft (9m) into Dryden Street. No. 43072 was cut up on site four days after the accident, but not officially withdrawn until the following month. *Ref:2197 (opposite) 2569 (above).*

Leeds City

The 2.40pm Leeds-Scarborough service would be late arriving on 10 August 1961, when the two four-car Class 101 units met with 'Peak' Class 45 No. D105 almost opposite Leeds East Signal Box. The leading two DMU vehicles (DMBS No. 51440 and TCL No. 59533) overturned. The leading motor coach (51440) turned over and slid on its side, demolishing the parapet wall of a bridge and releasing fuel oil that then ignited. The second coach (59533) also fell on its side, but the remaining six coaches were little damaged. All the DMU vehicles were repaired and returned to traffic. The locomotive was virtually new, being built at Crewe two months earlier; it too was repaired and worked until withdrawn as No. 45064 in July 1985. As well as damage to the rolling stock, the impact caused the bridge parapet to collapse, resulting in damage to property and road vehicles parked below. The report into the accident shows that the driver of the locomotive mis-read the signal that had been cleared for the DMU. The official report into the accident was conducted by Col. D McMullen of the Ministry of Transport who reported the diesel unit had been carrying 150 passengers. One passenger was killed in the accident and two others suffered shock. Clearly the local news photographers were quickly on the scene including one man with a camera on the roof of one of the vehicles in the lower view. (His head is cut-off on the original print.)
Ref: 1330 (top), 1344 (bottom).

Accidents

Knottingley

Locomotive in your living room...?
Class J39 No. 64705 appears to have run through the points at Knottingley on 6 September 1960 whilst shunting the yard. The engine had recently been reallocated from Ardsley (56B) to Wakefield (56A) and was based at the latter location from June 1960 to March 1961. The breakdown train crew have arrived with the depot's steam crane and are awaiting instructions prior to returning the locomotive to the rails. *Ref:1741.*

Bottom: Proving that the show must go on, a DMU is being sqeezed through the tight gap between the steam crane and derailed locomotive probably at less than walking pace. With comparatively little damage sustained in the derailment, No. 64705 survived in traffic for a further 18 months. *Ref:1686.*

Mansfield

Opposite: On 2 September 1950 the 9.18am three-coach passenger train from Nottingham (Victoria) to Edwinstowe was travelling at about 35 to 40mph (48-65km/h), when it became totally derailed on plain straight track about a mile and a half beyond Mansfield

Station. Fortunately the train was only very lighted loaded with just three passengers and none of these were injured – nor indeed was the guard. Similarly fortunate were the driver and fireman who remained on the footplate and so had a lucky escape. The tank locomotive and two leading coaches overturned down a 10ft (3m) embankment, the rear coach remained on the formation tilted over at an angle. Eighty yards of track were destroyed, a further 30 yards (27m) were distorted, and the superstructure of a small under-bridge was badly damaged by the derailed train. The train was headed by LNER Class N7 0-6-2T No. 69552. The breakdown trains have arrived to salvage carriages and locomotive behind two unidentified 4-6-0s. No. 69552 was built by Beyer, Peacock, Manchester, in March 1925 and withdrawn in May 1960. *Ref:2050.*

Mirfield

Above: Built at Darlington Works in September 1942 as part of the war effort, LNER 'V2' class locomotive No 3666 (BR No. 60954) was allocated to York (North) MPD, its one and only shed during its service. On 7 January 1962 No. 60954 over ran the buffer stops while working a freight train at Mirfield, ending up on its side. It is seen here after its train and tender had been removed. Sustaining comparatively little damage it was returned to the rails and visited Darlington Works for a heavy overhaul. Returned to service it was withdrawn less than two years later on 18 November 1963, being broken up at Darlington the following month. *Ref:1727.*

Tollerton

On 5 June 1950 the 12.15pm express passenger train from Newcastle to York was derailed about four miles south of Tollerton; consisting of seven coaches it was running at about 45mph (72km/h). It was reported that due to the hot weather the track had buckled under a previous express that was running at 65mph (105km/h) that, fortunately, was not derailed. Nine passengers and the driver and fireman of the 12.15pm express were injured; they were removed with the minimum of delay by ambulance to a hospital in York but were not detained. The remaining passengers, numbering about 100, were taken into York by special buses.

Left: The train locomotive, Class A1 No. 60153 *Flamboyant*, ended up in the cess with the train scattered over all four tracks. Nearest the camera a Thompson 'B1' class 4-6-0 has arrived with a breakdown crane and supporting crew and mess coaches. The other assisting locomotive cannot be identified. The somewhat 'bent' railway carriage, across all four lines, shows the lack of crash-worthiness of wooden-bodied rolling stock. *Ref:1708.*

Below: Photographed from the other direction, this side of the carriage has survived, but shows that the under frame has taken the brunt of the impact of the adjacent vehicles. The breakdown train crew are removing the coach bogies that have ended up inverted. The Gresley-designed Vestibule Third Corridor, No. 12084, was withdrawn in August, being beyond economic repair. *Ref:1486.*

Wath

The accident involving an empty coal train at Wath illustrates the fact that even as late as the 1950s, many wagons were fitted with wooden underframes *(above Ref:1998)* that had little structural integrity when subjected to unexpected events. Wagons identified in this pile up include examples from the London Midland and Southern Regions along with former Private Owner wagons. The Railway Inspectorate did not issue reports on accidents involving only freight trains, unless a fatality amongst railway staff was involved and such events were subject only to an internal investigation few reports of which have survived. *Ref:2000.*

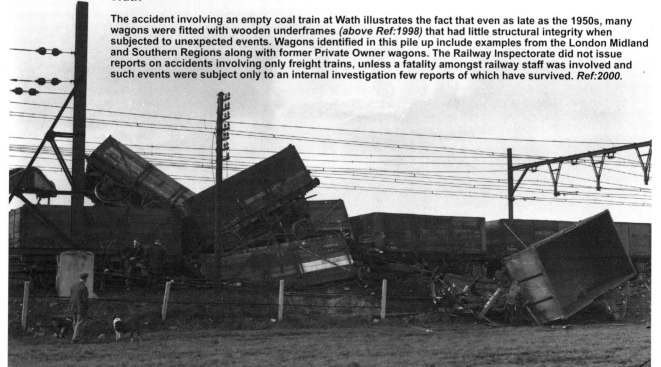

Winsford

On 17 April 1948, Stanier Class 8P No. 6251 *City of Nottingham* was hauling a mail train when it was in a rear-end collision with a passenger train at Winsford, Cheshire. This was the first major accident for the newly formed British Railways.

The two trains concerned were the 5.40pm Up express from Glasgow to Euston, comprising 10 bogie coaches, and the 6.25pm Up Postal express from Glasgow to Euston, composed of 13 bogie vans. The passenger train had been standing for about 17 minutes in the short section between Winsford Junction and Winsford station signal boxes after a passenger had pulled the communication cord. The collision was the result of the signalman at Winsford station subsequently accepting the Postal train although he had not seen the passenger train pass the box. The result was the Postal service, hauled by No 6251, running into the rear of the passenger train at between 40-45mph (64-72km/h). With both lines blocked, additional damage was averted with a Down Postal express being stopped at Winsford station box. The impact demolished the rear coach of the passenger train and half of the coach next ahead; there was also severe telescoping between the second, third and fourth vans of the Postal train. The passenger train was heavily loaded and sadly there were a number of fatalities – all in the last two coaches. Fourteen passengers and four of the Post Office staff were detained in hospital, of whom eight were discharged within a week, and twelve passengers and the two guards were treated for minor injuries or shock. Serious damage to the locomotive of the Postal train was confined to the front end, although the driver and fireman were uninjured. No. 6251 was repaired and returned to service until withdrawal in October 1964. *Ref:2054 (top), 2056 (bottom).*

York Locomotive Yard

As if to emphasise that not all accidents involve speed, the notice in the centre of the image reads 'Notice to Enginemen – Speed in this Loco Yard Not to Exceed Walking Pace'. On 3 March 1962 LNER 'A3' class No. 60075 *St Frusquin* has met with Trailer Second No. 59201 – the centre vehicle of a three-car Birmingham RC&W Class 104 unit. Not much damage was incurred by either party – the DMU returned to service, being withdrawn in May 1982. No. 60075 entered service in October 1924, being rebuilt from 'A1' to 'A3' in June 1942. Named after St Frusquin, a British racehorse that had a racing career lasting from May 1895 to July 1896, winning nine out of eleven races. Three wins in 1896 included the 2000 Guineas, the Princess of Wales's Stakes and Eclipse Stakes. No. 60075 was withdrawn in January 1964. *Ref:2423 (top), 2424 (bottom).*

Roadrailers

Opposite: The 'Roadrailer' was a bi-modal transportation unit, which could run as a semi-trailer on road and as a wagon on rail. The loaded trailers were filled at the factory, transported to the nearest railhead and moved by rail. The unit (with wheels attached as in a normal truck) would be moved by rail and decoupled from the wagon at the receiving end; then attached to a truck to be moved and taken to its final destination. The Roadrailers could provide door-to-door service by integrating the speed and efficiency of the railways with the flexibility of a road truck. In September 1960 BR trialled the use of this system; in 1963 a 41-wagon train was successfully run on the East Coast main line. Unfortunately it was claimed to be uneconomical, mainly through the logistical problems of removing intermediate wagons during the course of a journey, which, with the rise of the motorways around the UK, was not surprising. Perhaps improved marshalling at the start might have been the obvious solution. The system was of more use in countries where trains travelling long distances were the norm. Similar systems have been used in Australia and America (with over 7,000 RoadRailer units in operation with 14 terminal locations across the Eastern US and Canada at one time). In 2017 the hindubusinessline.com reported that trials were underway on the Chennai Division of the Southern Railway in India to operate a similar idea in a bid to divert cargo traffic from road to rail. *Ref:1336 (top), 1340 (bottom).*

Wagon Exhibition

The photographer has captured three newly constructed wagons for an exhibition of rolling stock, catalogue numbers 19, 20 and 21 according to the labels. The right-hand vehicle (with the identification '19' on a board at the right hand end), B885223, is a 20ton grain hopper – used for handling agricultural traffic and based on an original LMS design. Catalogue number 20 (centre vehicle) is a 'Covhop', No. B886655; BR introduced a standardised design of covered hopper wagon in 1952 and built over 1,000 up to 1961. They carried powders that could unload by gravity, usually without assistance – although some devices to lift and shake them were fitted to many. The final wagon is a 'Presflo' branded for the carriage of Pulverite – which is a sedimentary rock composed of silt- or clay-sized aggregates. These wagons were gravity loaded, but emptied using a compressed air supply to assist with the unloading. Almost 2,000 of these wagons were built, many being for the carriage of cement powder, and these were branded accordingly. *Ref:1034.*

The factory began production in 1884 as a planned expansion and replacement of the NER's Queen Street site; the works was substantially expanded in 1897-1900, and saw further modernisations through the 20th century. The works passed to the ownership of the LNER at the Grouping in 1923; British Railways in 1948. Then as British Rail Engineering Limited (BREL), which was incorporated on 31 October 1969, as the railway system's engineering subsidiary of BR until the design and building of trains in the UK was privatised in 1989.

Acquired by ABB (ASEA Brown Boveri, a Swiss-Swedish multinational corporation headquartered in Zurich, Switzerland). The works closed in 1996, due to lack of orders caused by uncertainty in the post-privatisation of BR period. From 1997 Thrall Car Manufacturing Co used the works to manufacture freight wagons for English Welsh & Scottish Railway, the first being delivered in 1998 continuing until 2002 when EWS policy changed; with the factory closing in 2003. Network Rail later acquired the main building in 2009 for storage and maintenance of Rail Head Treatment Trains that are used nationwide during the leaf fall season.

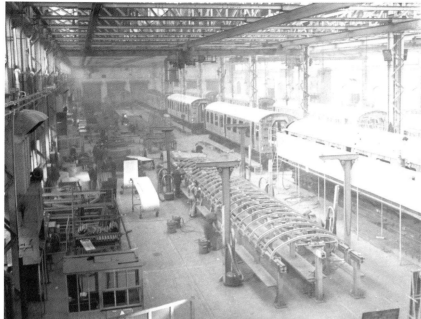

British Railways' first design of carriages were given the designation 'Mark 1', it was to be the standard coach design for use across all lines incorporating the best features of each of the former 'Big Four' companies. It was also designed to be much stronger than previous designs to provide better protection for passengers in the event of an accident. There were over 30 variants covering passenger stock, Pullmans, sleeping cars, Post Office and other non-passenger carrying vehicles. Having a separate body and under frame, it had a standard length of 64ft 6in (19.65m) or short 57ft (17.37m) frames for more restricted routes. The steel bodies were made from five jig-built sub-assemblies. The complete set of panels for a coach side were butted together and carbon arc welded, by machine on a roller table. (left). The sides had a 'tumblehome' and were fitted with flat windows; the curved shape also enabling slightly more room for passengers at shoulder level when seated. The roofs were assembled in a different part of the works before being assembled, and the complete ensemble being fitted to the chassis. These images were taken in the works in January 1954. *Ref:1624 (opposite page), 1626 (left).*

Buffet Car

The interior of a BR Mk 1 buffet car, designated as RMB – an Open Second with Miniature Buffet (also known as a Restaurant Miniature Buffet) – at an exhibition of the 'new' rolling stock. The first 12 vehicles, Nos. 1801-1812, were built at York between January and May 1958. Several of these vehicles are now in preservation, though over the years the interiors were often refurbished to a more modern style of decoration. When new they were fitted with a propane-fired Stills boiler for the supply of hot water. *Ref:1036.*

Chapter 6
Steam on Shed

Holbeck Locomotive Shed

Leeds was once a hotbed of locomotive sheds, with buildings at Copley Hill (GNR), subsequently relocated; Wortley (GNR and L&Y), later rebuilt at Wortley Junction; Hunslet Goods (GNR); Hunslet Lane (L&YR and NMR); Marsh Lane (L&SR) later relocated; Central, Low Level (GNR); Central Station (LNER); New Station (NER); Wellington (L&BR); and Holbeck – both the Leeds & Thirsk and Midland had sheds here! The images shown here are of the Holbeck (Midland Railway) shed, located to the south of Leeds City station. With a double roundhouse and concrete coaling tower the shed, coded 20A by BR (London Midland Region) from 1948-1957, housed 95 locomotives in September 1950. Transferred to the North Eastern Region – coded 55A, from 1957-1967 – it housed 81 locomotives in March 1959, and 40 in April 1965. Closure to steam came on 2 October 1967, with the shed being demolished. The repair shop was converted to a diesel depot, with a diesel servicing shed later erected on the site. For complete history details, readers are referred to *The Directory of British Engine Sheds* (see Bibliography).

With the concrete coaling tower dominating the view, Stanier-designed 'Jubilee' class 4-6-0 No. 45659 *Drake* has taken coal and is waiting for its next duty. Built at Derby in December 1934, it was allocated to Holbeck between September 1950 and June 1963. In the adjacent road, Hughes/Fowler Class 4MT No. 42759 (Crewe, June 1927) is also ready for departure. *Ref:1232.*

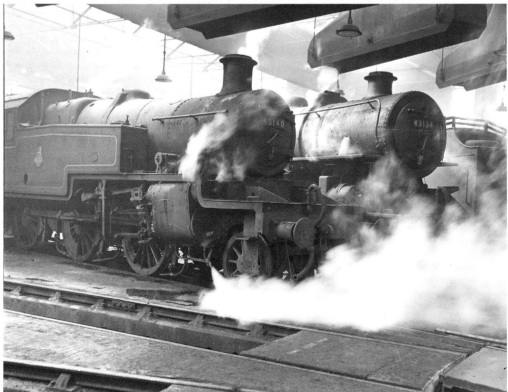

Dappled by the sun streaming through the sky-lights are Stanier-designed Class 3MT 2-6-2T No. 40140 (built at Derby in October 1935, withdrawn November 1961) and Ivatt-designed Class 4MT 2-6-0 No. 43124 (Horwich September 1951 / December 1966). Holbeck was the 'home' shed of both locomotives between September 1957 and October 1961. *Ref:1270.*

Chapter 7
The Derwent Valley Light Railway

The Derwent Valley Light Railway (DVLR) remained in private ownership following Nationalisation despite connections with British Railways at both ends. It ran between Layerthorpe on the outskirts of York to Cliffe Common near Selby. The southern end of the railway, from Wheldrake to Cliffe Common, was opened on 29 October 1912, with the remainder of the line opening on 19 July 1913. Although it was constructed primarily as a freight line, passenger trains were introduced from 1913. The North Eastern Railway used the line as a diversionary route between York and Selby during World War 1. In 1923, most British railway companies were grouped into four large companies, with the nearby North Eastern Railway becoming part of the London & North Eastern Railway. However, the DVLR remained independent, and continued to do so even after nationalisation in 1948. In 1964, British Railways closed the Selby-Driffield line, meaning that the junction at Cliffe Common became redundant. With the connection to Selby now gone, the DVLR was left isolated at its southern end. The line subsequently ran from Layerthorpe (York) but traffic generated by the southern section of the track was light so the decision was taken to close the line between Wheldrake and Cliffe Common in 1965. The section between Wheldrake and Elvington followed in 1968. Elvington was closed in 1973, leaving only approximately 4 miles (6.4km) of track between Layerthorpe and Dunnington on the outskirts of York. A regular summer steam passenger service commenced for three years in 1977, the first since closure to passengers in September 1926. Final closure to all freight traffic came on 27 September 1981 when the final train ran. In 1993 a short section was reopened as part of the Yorkshire Museum of Farming at Murton.

Between 1929 and 1969 the line was worked using hired in main line locomotives. Here Class 03 No D2112 is seen at Elvington at the head of a short train of two hopper wagons and a box van along with the DVLR's six-wheel brake van. In 1969 the DVLR acquired three British Railways Class 04 204hp diesel shunters. Two, Nos D2298 and D2245, were put into traffic with the third, No. D2392, stripped for spares before being recycled. *Ref:1907.*

Railway Memories

Above: Elvington some seven miles south east of York, looking towards the goods yard with a couple of rakes of mineral wagons visible. The area was well known for agricultural traffic, and as if to prove it a trailer load of sugar beet has arrived on the former platform. With war clouds gathering RAF Elvington was constructed nearby in 1939 and was in service from 1940 until 1992. Used as a bomber station, No.77 Squadron it suffered heavy losses of aircraft and flight crew during the Ruhr and Berlin campaigns; being replace by two French Squadrons in May 1944. The biggest change was postwar in 1952 when the original three runway layout was replace with a single 10,151ft (3,094m) one. Following abandonment by the United States Air Force in 1958 it was used as a relief landing ground for the RAF and test flights for the new Blackburn Buccaneer aircraft. Today part of the airfield is occupied by the Yorkshire Air Museum with several historic aircraft being in taxiable condition. *Ref:1917.*

Bottom: The station buildings were of a standard design with Wheldrake station being an example, which served the nearby village. This section of line closed to freight in 1968. The station building was dismantled and rebuilt at the Yorkshire Museum of Farming at Murton Park in 1997. The line gained its nickname of *The Blackberry Line* in the days when it used to transport blackberries to markets in Yorkshire and London. *Ref:1909.*

Opposite: The DVLR used a former South Eastern & Chatham Railway six-wheel brake van for sundries traffic. Acquired from the Southern Railway in 1946 and painted green, it was used until 1966 when replaced by a Pigeon Brake van, purchased from BR. The Station Master and Guard pass the time of day in March 1960. The SECR vehicle is now preserved on the Bluebell Railway. *Ref:1919.*

Chapter 8
Diesel Multiple Units

Whitby Town

(Opposite) Terminating at the coast, the station is at the end of a 30-mile (48km) line from Middlesbrough, the line follows the River Esk for much of its route. Opening between here and Grosmont in 1835, by the Whitby & Pickering Railway, the line was originally worked by horses, before being converted in 1845, in order to be able to accommodate steam locomotives, following a takeover by the York & North Midland Railway. In 1854, the line became a part of the NER. From Whitby Town, a single track branched up a steep incline to Prospect Hill Junction, from wh ch trains could reach Whitby West Cliff. From here trains would journey north along the coastal Whitby, Redcar & Middlesbrough Union Railway towards Staithes and Loftus, and south across the Larpool Viaduct towards Scarborough. The replacement for the original W&PR station at Whitby is seen here (top) following the arrival of a two-car Metro-Cammell DMU at platform 2, with the passengers queuing up to give their tickets to the ticket collector, a common sight at most railway stations at one time. A father is photographing his son (bottom) as the driver looks on. This is before rationalisation reduced the station to a single platform. Today the station is the eastern terminus for summer steam services over the heritage North Yorkshire Moors Railway. *Ref:2076 (top), 2074 (bottom).*

Derby Lightweights

The British Rail Derby Lightweight diesel multiple-units were the first such trains to be built en masse for British Railways. The units were built at BRs Derby Works from 1954 to 1955 and were assembled in various formations, including 12 power-twin 2-car units, 84 power-trailer 2-car units, and four 4-car units. Later two single car units were created from one two-car unit when passenger loadings reduced. Body framing was extruded and riveted together; with panelling being welded into continuous sheets and riveted to the frame. Luggage racks were manufactured from a light alloy. The floors had two layers of flameproof hardboard, covered with linoleum. To reduce noise and condensation, the inside structure and undersides were sprayed with asbestos (the danger not being appreciated at the time). Lighting was by 60-watt, 24-volt lamps charged by belt driven dynamos; with heating by using the train's diesel fuel supply. The mild steel bogies ran on Timken roller bearings. These sets were used as guinea pigs, testing out ideas for future DMUs. Their upkeep and maintenance was poor and the riveted body construction was easily damaged; in 1964 the original eight units were withdrawn from traffic. One of the first power-twins to be delivered, Nos. 79001 and 79501, was allocated to Bradford Hammerton Street and made various outings around Bradford and Leeds in early 1954. The person clad in white overalls would have been one of the technical team supervising the operation of the unit. These images show the unit at Bradford Exchange, unfortunately the date was not recorded. Despite the units having been constructed with electric lights, the traffic department insisted that traditional steam locomotive oil lamps be carried. *Ref:2084 (top left), 2086 (top right), 2088 (bottom left), 2090 (bottom right).*

Withernsea line

Above: One advantage of the first generation multiple units was the fact that, driver permitting, it was possible to see the route ahead – or behind. Here is the view from the passenger compartment of a Cravens unit on the Withernsea line. Introduced in 1959 all the vehicles were with drawn by the end of 1969. The Withernsea line, built by the Hull & Holderness Railway across the South Holderness area was easy to construct and opened to traffic between Withernsea and Hull (Victoria Dock) station on 30th June 1854. DMUs commenced operation on 7 January 1957, but was not enough to save the line from closure. The Hull-Withernsea line closed to passenger traffic on 19th October 1964 – the same day as the Hull-Hornsea service. Goods traffic as far as Heden continued until 3rd June 1968. The image was taken before hi-visibility clothing has been invented, the track crew are dressed in everyday work wear. *Ref:1843.*

The Easingwold Railway

Opposite: The Easingwold Railway had a long gestation period; first proposed in 1836 it was not until 23 August 1887 that a consortium of local businessmen formed the Easingwold Railway Co and obtained parliamentary approval to build the line. The unfortunately named contractor, Death & Co, went bust during construction; with a replacement contractor found the line opened on 27 July 1891 at a cost of £17,000.The line was privately owned throughout its period of operation and made small profits for most of that time. By 1920, the Easingwold was paying a regulardividend of about 3-4% before road competition began to effect railway traffic. The line, running 2.5 miles (4km) from Alne (on the NER's York-Northallerton line) to Easingwold; it remained an independent railway throughout its history, not passing to either the LNER or BR. It fell victim to road competition in the late 1940s and passenger services ended on 29 November 1948, with freight services ending with the line's closure on 30 December 1957. The first locomotive was a Hudswell Clarke 0-4-0ST, works No. 342, this was purchased on 24 of June 1891. For some reason the Board of Trade objected to the use of four-coupled locomotives. Its replacement was Hudswell Clarke 0-6-0ST, works No 334, which worked until sold in 1903. A third Hudswell Clarke locomotive, works No 608, was supplied on 7 May 1903. More powerful than the previous two locomotives, it made brief returns to Hudswell Clarke for overhauls and repairs. An older 0-6-0ST, named *Trent*, was used in September 1924 when 608 went for repairs, this locomotive survived until 1948/49 but was scrapped at Darlington when it arrived for a new firebox and boiler in 1947. Rather than replace the locomotive the decision was taken to hire in locomotives from the LNER (later BR). Typically these were ageing 'J71' and 'J72' 0-6-0Ts, the latter being illustrated here. The first set of coaches was two 26ft (7.9m) NER four-wheelers. Replacements came in 1932, in the shape of three ex-North London Railway carriages dating from 1872, two composites and a brake third/luggage van with birdcage lookout were used on passenger duties. They in turn were replaced by two NER six-wheelers that lost their centre wheels for use on the ELR; but both were replaced in the 1930s by an NER six-wheeler. In 1946, the NER six-wheeler was replaced by a Manchester, Sheffield & Lincolnshire Railway six-wheel brake composite that was employed on passenger workings; this carriage is now preserved on the Chasewater Railway. Goods stock was always supplied by the NER and its successors. *Ref:2215.*

Chapter 9
Easingwold Railway

The photographer did not record the locomotive number, or date, when he visited the line. This view taken at Easingwold illustrates the driver climbing aboard the 'J72' and the MS&LR brake composite. *Ref:2215.*

An overall view of the station at Easingwold, note the raised siding on the right that enabled coal to be dropped to the ground, saving on manpower. The wooden station building and empty platform are also visible. *Ref:2219.*

Chapter 10

Locomotives for Export

Hudswell, Clarke & Co Ltd

In 1860 William S Hudswell founded the company, having served his apprenticeship with Kitson & Co, with John Clarke, the work's manager from the same company, as an engineering and locomotive builder. In 1866 Mr Rodgers joined the organisation and in 1870 the company name was changed to Hudswell, Clarke & Rodgers. The name reverted to Hudswell, Clarke & Co in 1880 when Rodgers left the company. During World War 2 the company diversified into armaments, as did so many other engineering companies. In the post-war period the company was closely involved in many secret programmes, including the British nuclear weapon project. The company manufactured the airframe for the first British nuclear bomb, Blue Danube; the airframe for Red Beard, the second-generation tactical nuclear bomb, followed with that for Violet Club, the interim megaton weapon; and there were many other projects. All the bombs detonated at the Christmas Island H-bomb tests were contained in airframes designed and built by the company. In 1961 the last steam locomotive left the works, the company having constructed 1,807 in the 101 years of the company's existence.

Locomotive building was always only one part of a diverse product inventory that included underground diesel-powered mining locomotives, hydraulic pit props and related mining equipment. The company also contributed to other military projects, e.g. the Centurion main battle tank conversion into an armoured bridge-layer, which served with the British Army for many years; the contraction of defence manufacturing in the mid-1960s contributed to the sale and demise of the company.

In 1937 the newly elected New Zealand government launched a major programme of investment by the creation of the Public Works Department, and as a result placed an order with Hudswell Clarke for 12 diesel locomotives. Allocated Works Nos D591-602, at the time this was the largest order of diesels the company had received. Delivered in 1937 these four-wheel locomotives had a maximum speed of 9mph (14.5km/h). The 3ft 6in (1.07m) gauge locomotives had low-height cabs enabling them to be carried on railway wagons to where they were required. Four eventually went to the main line operator in the country where they were fitted with taller cabs. *Ref:2518*.

Hunslet Engine Co

The company was founded in 1864 at Jack Lane, Hunslet, Leeds, by John Towlerton Leather, a civil engineering contractor, who appointed James Campbell as his Works Manager. The first locomotive, built in 1865, was *Linden*, an 0-6-0ST delivered to Brassey & Ballard, a railway civil engineering contractor, as were several of the firm's early customers. This basic standard gauge shunting and short haul 'industrial' locomotive was to be the mainstay of Hunslet production for many years. The first locomotive built for export was Works No. 10, an 0-4-0ST shipped to Java. By 1902, Hunslet had supplied locomotives to over 30 countries worldwide, often opening up new markets. In Ireland, it supplied locomotives to several of the newly opened narrow gauge lines and, also in 1887, built the three unorthodox 0-3-0 locomotives for the Lartigue Monorail system used by the Listowel & Ballybunion Railway. In 1902, the company was reorganised as a private limited company with the name Hunslet Engine Co Ltd. – but was still a family business. Not unexpectedly during World War 1 overseas orders dried up and the company, like many others, found itself employing women on the shop floor and was also engaged in the manufacture of munitions. It continued to produce limited numbers of locomotives, significant examples being lightweight narrow gauge 4-6-0T designs for the War Department Light Railways. Post-war Hunslet were once more able to attract overseas customers; they also received a series of repeat orders from the LMS for 90 Class 3F 0-6-0T shunting locomotives. As independent British manufacturers failed to survive the depression of the 1920s and 1930s, it acquired the patterns, rights and designs of other builders including Kerr, Stuart and the Avonside Engine Co. Throughout the 1930s, Hunslet worked on the perfecting of diesel traction. During World War 2, the company again served the country in the manufacture of munitions, but they also built locomotives, both steam and diesel, for the war effort. Noteworthy is their role in the production of the 'Austerity' 0-6-0ST shunting locomotive; with a total of 485 built by them and other builders from 1943. An important post-war product was the flameproof diesel locomotive for use in the coal mines, as well as further batches of Austerity shunters for the National Coal Board and the Army; the final examples emerging in 1964. The last industrial steam locomotive built in Britain was erected at Jack Lane in 1971 for export to the Trangkil sugar mill in Central Java, Indonesia. The Jack Lane, Hunslet, works was closed in 1995, the last order being a batch of narrow gauge diesel locomotives for tunnelling on the Jubilee Line extension of the London Underground. In 2004 the Hunslet Engine Co was acquired by the LH Group Services and is now part of the Wabtec Corporation.

With the cab windows and some of the other apertures covered, this Hunslet-built 0-8-0 diesel-mechanical is bound for the Mufulira Copper Mines in Northern Rhodesia in 1955. Fitted with a Paxman 12RPHL Series 2 engine, and Hunslet two-speed automatic gearbox, the locomotive weighed in at 56 tons. The engine was de-rated from its usual 500bhp rating to 440bhp at 1,250rpm for the local high altitude (4,000ft/1,219m) and ambient temperature (95°F/35°C) conditions. To the right of the locomotive, one of what became the BR Class 05 0-6-0DM shunters is under construction. *Ref:1749.*

Yorkshire Engine Co

W G Eden, who was Chairman of the South Yorkshire Railway, and a director of the Manchester, Sheffield & Lincolnshire Railway, first suggested the idea of a locomotive builder based near Sheffield in 1864. The company was formed in 1865 and the first order received was for three 2-2-2 locomotives for the GNR. Demand for new locomotives tailed off and in order to keep the workforce together, other work was undertaken, including armour plated shields, lampposts for Sheffield, and 10,000 safes. The building of locomotives to Robert Fairlie's patent started at the end of 1871. Between 1872 and 1883, 13 were supplied to the Mexican Railway in three batches. These were double-ended 0-6-6-0 machines; the middle batch had Walschaerts valve gear, believed to be the first time that this design was used in Britain. The Mexican locomotives were capable of burning coal or wood as a fuel, while two supplied to Sweden burnt peat. The peat burners were not a success and were rebuilt as four 2-4-0 saddle tanks. An order for 10 Fairlies received in 1873 for nitrate railways in Peru were built, but were not shipped because payment was not received. Instead four went to the Transcaucasian Railway near the Black Sea, and six were shipped to the recently formed Nitrate Railways Ltd, Chile, in 1882. They had a 2-6-6-2 wheel arrangement, and weighed in at 85 tons each; *Engineering* reported that they were the heaviest locomotives in the world in 1885. The collieries and steelworks of Yorkshire were regular customers. The 1890s saw the YEC building locomotives for Chile, Peru and India. During 1907 the company started to build motorcars, branded as 'YEC'. These were not a success and very few were produced. YEC also undertook orders for main line locomotives for the UK and overseas countries; 1928 saw the LNER getting deliveries directly from Sheffield. These nine locomotives (LNER Nos. 2682-2690) were Class N2 0-6-2Ts for working suburban trains. Along with a number of other private builders, YEC built a batch of GWR '5700' class 0-6-0PTs in 1929/1930. Between 1949 and 1956, 50 GWR-design '9400' class 0-6-0PTs were built for BR. The last of these, BR No. 3409 (YE2584 of 1956), was the last steam locomotive built at Meadowhall and the last BR locomotive to be built to a pre-nationalisation design. The United Steel Companies Ltd (USC) bought the business on 29 June 1945. USC needed replacement locomotives so it made sense to buy a manufacturer; the idea had been put forward of developing a central engineering workshop for their steelworks at Templeborough (Rotherham) and Stocksbridge. Both works were being expanded and redeveloped, being easily accessible by rail from the YEC works. Following the purchase, work began on building locomotives for the internal rail systems at several steelworks as well as ironstone mines around Britain. Steam locomotives were built from 1865 to 1956 and diesel locomotives from 1950 to 1965 when locomotive construction ceased.

In 1953 the YEC built a pair of 2-6-0s (Work Nos 2513/14) for the Ferrocarril Presidente Carlos Antonio López in Paraguay; these were based on a North British Locomotive Co design but with higher pitched boilers with increased pressure. The 234-mile line linked the country's Capital, Asunción with Encarnación, where a ferry connection was made with the Urqiza Railway in Argentina. Construction of the line commenced in 1861 through the initiative of President López, during a period of state inspired development. Originally laid to 5ft 6in (1.67m) gauge it was rebuilt as standard gauge in 1911 in order to conform to the Argentine line. Note that the locomotive is supplied complete with number and nameplates, No 152 *Ascunsión*. The other locomotive supplied was No 151 *Encarnación*. The wooden 'crate' on the boiler covers a bell, no doubt to avoid corrosion during the sea voyage, like wise the cab and remaining motion and bearings are protected. The rods would have been protected and probably shipped strapped to the tender. *Ref:1512*.

Chapter 11

Industrial

Dunlop & Ranken

Above: With the registered office located at 147 The Headrow, in the Farnley area of Leeds, Dunlop & Ranken were iron and steel stockholders, and claimed to hold 'Huge Stocks for Immediate delivery'. As with a lot of steel girder suppliers the end product was rolled with the company name incorporated. The labels on the end of the wagon read 'Steel from Dunlop & Ranken Ltd Leeds Stockyards', the location is Liversedge Spen – the site of a later oil terminal – and is believed to have been taken during World War 2. George Cohen, Sons & Co acquired the company in January 1956 – becoming part of the 600 Group it was sold to the British Steel Corporation in 1980.
Ref:1358.

Harrogate Gas Works

Harrogate Gas Co was formed in 1845 and obtained an Act of Parliament in 1846. The works were situated at Rattle Crag on the main Ripon road. Prior to 1880 coal was carted from Starbeck, three miles away. In 1908-1909, a light railway was constructed from Bilton sidings to the gasworks and locomotives were purchased by the gas company (Gas Light Co). The works were enlarged again in 1908-1909 and in 1911. In 1925 the Harrogate GC took over the Pateley Bridge GC whose works were at Glasshouses. In 1927 Harrogate GC extended its area of supply again by absorbing the Tadcaster and Wetherby GLC, the Boston Spa GC, the gas undertaking of Knaresborough UDC and the Boroughbridge GLC; the offices of the Harrogate GC were improved and enlarged in 1928-1929 following the rapid expansion of the company's area. Workshops were also developed at Cambridge Street. In 1936 the United Kingdom GC obtained a controlling interest in the company, which became part of the York, Harrogate & District

Group of Gas Companies. On nationalisation in 1949 the undertaking became part of the Harrogate / York Group of the North East Gas Board. Built by Thomas Green & Sons (works No. 441) in 1908, *Barber* was a 2ft gauge 0-6-2ST and fitted with a round-top cab in order to fit the limited loading gauge of the Harrogate line. The driver is cleaning his charge when photographed, sometime before the locomotive was withdrawn in 1949. Following preservation, the locomotive is now on the South Tynedale Railway and following extensive, and expensive, restoration work was restored to steam in 2014. *Ref:1706.*

Esholt Sewage Works

The Esholt Sewage Works Railway was a standard gauge works railway constructed in 1910 to serve the works in Esholt, West Yorkshire; built and owned by the Waterworks Department of Bradford Corporation (which also owned the Nidd Valley Light Railway as many of the corporation's largest reservoirs were constructed beyond Pateley Bridge). The branch line was connected to the Midland Railway's Leeds & Bradford line, leaving as a northerly spur west of Apperley Bridge station and east of Thackley Tunnel. The spur left the main line immediately east of the rail bridge over the Leeds & Liverpool Canal with the branch and associated sidings staying, for the most part, to the east and north of the canal, and west and south of the river as both curve north of Thackley. Branches at Thackley Hill bridged both watercourses. The connection with the Midland line required a signal box and exchange sidings for the transfer of wagons between the two systems. The sewage works were built to remove wool grease and other wastes from effluent coming out of the many mills of the Bradford woollen district. At its peak, the railway extended to 22 miles (35km) of track served by 11 locomotives, as well as a shorter section of narrow gauge railway served by three locomotives. Trains were employed to remove solid waste from the site; several of the locomotives were converted to run on oil derived from recovered wool grease. The railway was closed completely in 1977; however the sewage works continues to operate.

On 12 October 1957 the Railway Correspondence & Travel Society organised a trip around the Esholt Sewage Works. The motive power for the trip was supplied by *Nellie*, an 0-6-0ST built by Hudswell Clarke (works No 1435) in 1922. *Nellie* was preserved at the Bradford Industrial Museum at Eccleshill upon withdrawal; and is currently on loan to the Embsay & Bolton Abbey Railway. *Ref:2098.*

Nellie again, this time providing an opportunity for the Auxiliary Fire Service (AFS) to practise – note the hoses beneath the rails! The AFS was formed in 1938 as part of the Civil Defence Service. Its role was to supplement the work of brigades at local level. The AFS and the local brigades were superseded in August 1941 by the National Fire Service. After the war the AFS was reformed alongside the Civil Defence Corps, forming part of the UK's planned emergency response to a nuclear attack. It was disbanded in 1968. *Ref:2100.*

Chapter 12

Staff at Work

The 'Fair Maid'

Top: One aspect of the main line railway companies was the policy of naming their important services. For a period in 1957/8 'The Fair Maid' was the name given to a morning London King's Cross to Perth service. This was a successor to the 'Morning Talisman' (King's Cross-Edinburgh Waverley and Glasgow Queen Street) that ran from 1957-1968. With no paint on the brush this is almost certainly a posed image. *Ref:1016.*

Tees-Thames Express

Left: The fireman of 'B1' class 4-6-0 No. 61255 puts up the express passenger train head code on 2 November 1959 for the inaugural run of the weekdays only 'Tees-Thames' from Saltburn, via Middlesbrough to King's Cross. This early morning service named train ceased running at the end of the summer timetable in 1961. The headboard was a homespun affair, probably wooden, made by either the station staff, or Thornaby shed staff that provided the locomotive. No. 61255 was built by the North British Locomotive Co in November 1947, being withdrawn in June 1967. *Ref:1026.*

Carriage cleaning at Neville Hill

One of many unsung jobs in the railway industry is that of the carriage cleaners. With brushes and an early vacuum cleaner in hand, these views were taken in the Neville Hill Carriage Shed. Walter Griffiths designed the first cleaning machine that used a vacuum, which could be carried around, in 1905. It used bellows to suck up dust and a flexible pipe. The vehicle on the left, No. 43150E, is a vestibule brake composite built to a Gresley design for the Great Northern Railway in 1909. After two centuries of carriage development there is a human element involved in the clearing of detritus left by the travelling public! *Ref:1680 (right), 2341 (bottom).*

Scrooby tracklaying

Regular track replacement was a day-to-day operation on the railway. Main line track had to be maintained to the highest standards as it was travelled over at high speed by heavy trains. For decades this was hard manual work, and, as can be seen here, the use of high-visibility jackets and hard hats were a long way into the future. On double track lines where total occupancy was available, once the track requiring replacement had been removed the new pre-assembled track was laid – generally in 45 or 60ft lengths (above). With the new track on the ground and connected up (centre), the PW gang is doing the initial alignment before ballast is dropped onto it. The levelling is done by eye (sometimes using levelling boards), with adjustment taking place with the use of jacks, and manually shovelling ballast under the sleepers. The ballast has been laid and final dressing and levelling is taking place; at this time there was plenty of manpower available (bottom). The location is thought to be near Scrooby to the south of Doncaster, on the East Coast main line; with Class 08 0-6-0DE shunter No. D3443, built at Doncaster in January 1957, allocated to Darnall depot in Sheffield upon delivery, hauling the PW train and equipment. No. D3443 was fitted with a non-standard power unit – a Blackstone ERT6 in place of the standard English Electric 6K – and was withdrawn from Healey Mills depot in July 1984. In the original image, 'dropped joints' – where the individual rails are connected by fishplates – on the other track are clearly visible. *Ref:1062 (top), 1058 (centre), 1056 (bottom).*

Chapter 13

Spurn Point Military Railway

Spurn Point had been militarised in 1805 during the Napoleonic Wars. When World War 1 was declared, the number of military personnel on Spurn Point increased greatly overnight. The War Department decided that a railway line between Kilnsea and Spurn Point would be the best option for a supply chain and so purchased the land required. The line was constructed by C J Wills & Co with rails and other second-hand materials from main line operators. The contractors also brought five standard gauge steam tank locomotives to help build the line, one of which was left behind to work the line. The line opened in 1915 with the rails extending onto the jetty at Spurn Point as it was isolated from the res of the mainland railway network. Rail transport was chosen as the roads in the area were narrow and twisting and supplies could be easily delivered by boat to the jetty, enabling transhipment of goods and materials to be supplied to the fortifications and batteries along the stretch of railway up to Kilnsea. The small locomotives operated most trains but some diesel and petrol railcars were used (top), especially after the only resident locomotive was scrapped in 1929. Local people who lived on Spurn Point used wind-power to 'sail' small homemade 'land ship' trolleys up and down the railway, with some notable crashes off the rails and into trains coming the other way. The railway was also home to an adapted Itala racing car with flanged wheels that was capable of going at 60 miles (97km/h) per hour. Guns were also transported along the line, with at least one incident where the train broke down at the narrowest point and the train was buffeted by the Humber on one side and the North Sea on the other. The line had a two-road locomotive shed, situated a short distance north of the lighthouse. The rails leading to it can be seen behind the railcar, the latter supplied by Hudswell Clarke in 1933, with the water supply tank to left of image (bottom). The line closed in 1951 as a post-war economy, being replaced by a road which, ironically, was built with materials brought in by the railway. Spurn Head was also demilitarised in stages between 1956 and 1959. *Ref:1426 (top), 2451 (bottom*

Chapter 11

The End

Above: Two of Gresley's finest awaiting the torch, following replacement by diesel traction, are seen awaiting recycling at Doncaster Works. 'A4' class Nos. 60014 *Silver Link* and 60028 *Walter K. Whigham* sit in the yard following withdrawal on 29 December 1962. No. 60028 would be scrapped in January 1963 and No. 60014 in August 1964. This area of the works was known as 'Burma Road'. Sir Billy Butlin (of holiday camp fame) was interested in obtaining a number of withdrawn steam locomotives for display at various camps and was interested in No. 60014. It was not to be, so Sir Billy obtained former LMS Pacifics for display; without this change of direction the heritage movement would be missing *Princess Margaret Rose, Duchess of Hamilton* and *Duchesss of Sutherland. Ref:1452.*

Opposite: The remains nearest the camera are probably that of 'A3' class No. 60068 *Sir Visto*, built by the North British Locomotive Co, entering traffic on 14 September 1924 and withdrawn on 27 August 1962; being cut up later the same month. The exercise was one of sorting the various types of metals for recycling, the nearest wagon to the left of the yard holding cast iron, with the other used for non-ferrous materials. The tubs on the left contain bearings and rods destined for recycling. *Ref:2508.*

Bibliography and Further Reading

Books:

A multitude of books were referred to when writing this book, the following proved to be useful sources of information:

Anon; *British Railways Atlas 1947 (2nd Edition) and RCH Junction Diagrams*, Ian Allan Publishing, 2016.
Bolger, Paul; *BR Steam Motive Power Depots: LMS*, 9780711010192, Ian Allan, 1981.
Bolger, Paul; *BR Steam Motive Power Depots: NER*, 9780711013629, Ian Allan, 1984.
Clinker, C. R.; *Clinker's Register of Closed Passenger Stations and Goods Depots in England, Scotland and Wales 1830-1977*, 0905466195, Avon Anglia, 1978.
Cobb, Col M. H.; *The Railways of Great Britain: A Historical Atlas (2nd Edn)*, 978071103236X, Ian Allan, 2006.
Griffiths, R. & Smith, P.; *The Directory of British Engine Sheds and Principal Locomotive Servicing Points: Vol 2*, 9780860935483, OPC, 2000.
Hartley, Kenneth E.; *The Spurn Head Railway*, Industrial Railway Record No 67, IRS, 1976.
Hendry, Robert; *British Railways Goods Wagons in Colour*, 978185780094X, Midland Publishing, 1999.
Joy, David; *A Regional History of the Railways of Great Britain: Vol 8 – South and West Yorkshire*; 07153688834, David & Charles, 1975.
Grant, Donald J.; *Directory of the Railway Companies of Great Britain*, 9781788037686, Matador, 2017.
Holland, Julian; *Dr Beeching's Axe – 50 Years On*, 9781446302675, David & Charles, 2013.
Longworth, Hugh; *British Railways First Generation DMUs*, 9780860936121, OPC, 2011.
Longworth, Hugh; *British Railways Steam Locomotives 1948-1968*, 9780860935933, OPC, 2005.
Longworth, Hugh; *British Railways Steam Locomotive Allocations*, 9780860936428, OPC, 2011.
Maboff, F. W., *Manning Wardle & Company Ltd – Locomotive Works List*, 0906829089, Thomas Aleksandr, 1981.
Marsden, C.J.; *DMU and EMU Recognition Guide*, 9780711037403, Ian Allan, 2013.
Marsden, Colin J.; *The Complete UK Modern Traction Locomotive Directory*, 9780955788789, TRC.Com Publishing, 2011.
Millar, Sean; *Hunslet & Hudswell Clarke Locomotives in New Zealand*, 9781927329184, Sean Millar Publishing, 2018.
Redman, Ronald Nelson; *Hudswell Clarke & Co Ltd: A Pictorial Album of Narrow Gauge Locomotives*, 0948131322, Trent Valley Publications, 1992.
Tuffrey, P. & Roe, M.; *150 Years of Doncaster Plant Works*, 9781872062044, Bond Publications & WabtecRail Ltd, 2003.
Walmsley, Tony; *Shed by Shed: Part 1, London Midland*, 9780956061553, St Petroc InfoPublishing, 2010.
Walmsley, Tony; *Shed by Shed: Part 3, North Eastern*, 9780956061539, St Petroc InfoPublishing, 2010.

Online
One of the richest sources of information, with sites covering disused stations, closing dates by year, and individual companies, etc. Perhaps the most interesting is the National Library of Scotland's Ordnance Survey collection, also of interest – disused-stations.org.uk – lner.info – also gracesguide.co.uk .

Memorial plaque on Bramhope Tunnel, Leeds.
Ref:1094.

THE
PERFECT START
to YOUR DAY

THE
PERFECT START
to YOUR DAY

NOURISHING & INDULGENT RECIPES FOR BREAKFAST & BRUNCH

TONIA GEORGE

photography by Jonathan Gregson

RYLAND PETERS & SMALL

LONDON • NEW YORK

Senior designer Megan Smith
Senior editor Céline Hughes
Head of Production Patricia Harrington
Creative director Leslie Harrington
Editorial director Julia Charles

Food stylist Tonia George
Prop stylist Liz Belton
Assistant food stylist Siobhan Boyle
Indexer Hilary Bird

Originally published in 2012. This
revised edition published in 2024 by
Ryland Peters & Small
20–21 Jockey's Fields
London WC1R 4BW
and
341 E 116th St
New York, NY 10029

www.rylandpeters.com

10 9 8 7 6 5 4 3 2 1

ISBN: 978-1-78879-602-6

A CIP record for this book is available
from the British Library.
US Library of Congress Cataloging-in-
Publication data has been applied for.

Printed and bound in China

MIX
Paper | Supporting
responsible forestry
FSC® C008047

Notes

• The recipes in this book are given in both
metric and imperial measurements plus US
cups for convenience. Please note that the
spellings are primarily British.
• All spoon measurements are level, unless
otherwise specified.
• Ovens should be preheated to the
specified temperature. Recipes in this
book were tested using a regular oven. If
using a fan oven, follow the manufacturer's
instructions for adjusting temperatures.
• Recipes containing raw or partially
cooked egg, or raw fish or shellfish, should
not be served to the very young, very
old, anyone with a compromised immune
system or pregnant women.
• Sterilize preserving jars before use.
Wash them in hot, soapy water and rinse
in boiling water. Place in a large saucepan,
then cover with hot water. With the lid on,
bring the water to the boil and continue
boiling for 15 minutes. Turn off the heat,
then leave the jars in the hot water until
just before they are to be filled. Invert
the jars onto clean kitchen paper to dry.
Sterilize the lids for 5 minutes, by boiling,
or according to the manufacturer's
instructions. Jars should be filled and
sealed while they are still hot.

Contents

Rise & shine!

Breakfast is by far and away my favourite meal of the day, which is ironic because mornings are probably my least favourite time of the day. Some days the thought of a frothy mocha and a slab of sourdough toast slathered in peanut butter is the only incentive there is to throw back the duvet and face the world.

And if it's difficult enough to force yourself out of bed, it's an even tougher job luring other grumpy heads out of their warm, cosy slumber. That must be why typical breakfast and brunch dishes are so full of vibrant flavours; salty bacon, sweet ambrosial maple syrup, creamy eggs, steaming coffee, voluptuous yogurt and zingy fruits. I defy anyone to sleep on contentedly once the smoky aromas of bacon frying and toast turning golden creep up their nostrils.

Some days the thought of a frothy mocha and a slab of toast slathered in peanut butter is the only incentive there is to throw back the duvet and face the world.

Rushing out of the house with an empty tummy is never a good idea. Miss breakfast and research shows that you're more likely to suffer poor concentration and a slump in energy levels. Eating also kickstarts your metabolism and stabilizes blood sugar levels, so skipping a meal in the hope of saving on a few calories is counterproductive. Armed with the many recipes in this book, there really is no excuse. There are lots of quick ideas for rushed weekday mornings when everything seems to conspire against letting you leave the house on time, from Nutty Honey Granola (page 33) and Rhubarb & Orange Compote (page 29), to a five-minute Banana, Honey & Wheatgerm Lassi (page 18) which can be wolfed down in a flash. Some you'll need to prepare on the weekend, but they promise to see you right through the week.

I have always been a huge fan of breakfast. When I was younger my mother made me toast before school every single morning – always one with Marmite and one with marmalade. If we were late for school the toast would be finished in the car. But when the weekend came around it was a different story. The whole family wandered about in their dressing gowns in a well-rehearsed formation, each with their own job: the chief toast maker, someone to make the coffee, and another at the stove turning slices of bacon and links of sausages until the table was groaning with food.

On birthdays and Mother's Day the mornings would stretch a little further, sometimes into the afternoon. After appetites had been whetted with Buck's Fizz, we would dig into bowls of Greek yogurt scattered with pecans, drizzled with honey and topped with chunks of tropical fruit. After a short break we'd be back for Blueberry Pancakes (page 89), light and fluffy enough to absorb twice their weight of maple syrup, or sometimes a buttery Smoked Haddock Kedgeree (page 113) hiding lovely chunks of fresh fish and still-soft boiled egg.

It's very insightful to see how people start their days. There are those that go for the sugar and caffeine rush of a coffee and a pastry, others who need a plateful of eggs and

Breakfast stirs up cosy, nostalgic memories evoking hearth and home, and having someone cook it for you makes you feel nurtured.

sausages alongside mountains of toast, and plenty of others still that dare not deviate from their more virtuous bowl of oats. I've included recipes to please all of you, from hurried weekday breakfasts to leisurely weekend brunches. In fact a weekend brunch is a good chance to try some of the more eclectic dishes. After the repetitive rhythm of the week, it's a time when I like to explore what other cultures eat. In England we've been doing this since the Victorian times, when kedgeree was introduced to the breakfast table from India. Likewise, in California, Huevos Rancheros (page 49) has now become a staple brunch fixture. There are many other dishes that I have borrowed for this book, such as Spain's delicious cinnamon sugar-coated Churros (page 78), and the Scandinavian Gravadlax (page 119), to modern Australian classics such as Corn Cakes with Bacon & Avocado (page 106) born of a love for fresh ingredients.

Of course, I'm very particular about what goes on my breakfast plate, and I find that most people are. Eggs must be cooked to perfection – for me this means they need to ooze with an ocherous yolk but for others any trace of wobble will have been left far behind. My bacon needs to be so crisp that it snaps, but you might find it too dry like this. And whereas some balk at the marriage of sweet maple syrup with smoky bacon, I couldn't imagine life without it. So feel free to adapt the recipes to suit your own set of foibles; that's exactly what makes us who we are.

More than any other meal, I've also noticed how breakfast turns grown adults back into fussy children. Look at the way people cling to their favourite childhood cereal all through their adult life, and never lose the wide-eyed pleasure at seeing a stack of pancakes dripping with butter. Breakfast stirs up cosy, nostalgic memories evoking hearth and home, and

having someone cook it for you makes you feel nurtured. This is what makes it a special meal.

I also find brunching to be a rather intimate ritual. Sharing your morning meal tends to be reserved for partners and family and so brunch is where friendships are cemented and intimate secrets spilled. You might breakfast alone, but it's never okay to brunch alone. Perhaps this is the only real difference in breakfasting and brunching, because after all, when exactly does a breakfast become a brunch? Does it depend on what, when or how much you eat? Is anything more than three slices of toast after noon considered brunch? There is no definitive answer. The actual term was recorded by Guy Beringer in his visionary article 'Brunch: A plea' published in *Hunter's Weekly* in 1895. He makes a case for replacing the post-hunt meal with a multi-course feast starting with more breakfast-friendly fare. 'Brunch is cheerful, sociable and

compelling… and sweeps away the worries and cobwebs of the week', he wrote. It caught on in affluent social circles, but wasn't fully embraced until it crossed the Atlantic in the 1930s, where it took off as an indulgent Mother's Day treat.

Even now 'doing brunch' implies a certain amount of hedonism. Stretching the morning meal into the afternoon hours usually comes about after an eventful evening which has encroached upon your night of sleep. This is what feels so decadent about brunch. It defies convention and is full of contradictions: you can ignore alarm clocks, eat something sweet before your savoury course, enjoy cake before noon and have a cocktail alongside a boiled egg. It is truly a time when you can do what you want to rather than what you should do – a sentiment that very much appeals as I roll over, smile contentedly and switch off my bleeping alarm clock on a Saturday morning.

drinks

Carrot, apple & ginger juice Pear, kiwi & apple juice **Basil limeade**
Pineapple & mint agua fresca Pomegranate & orange sunrise **Banana,
honey & wheatgerm lassi** Cashew nut & mango smoothie Raspberry,
strawberry & orange juice **Bloody mary** Sea breeze Blood orange &
campari mimosa **Lemon & sage tisane** Real hot chocolate Spiced mocha

Carrot, apple & ginger juice

4 carrots
2 apples, quartered
3 cm/1 ½ in. fresh ginger
ice, to serve
juicer
SERVES 2

There is something about this blend of fruit and vegetables that feels so extremely virtuous and cleansing. It is very thirst-quenching as well, especially when served really well chilled. Great for a hangover.

Pass the carrots, apples and ginger
through a juicer, one at a time, into a jug.
Add enough ice for 2 people and serve.

Pear, kiwi & apple juice

3 pears, quartered
3 kiwi fruit, quartered
1 apple, quartered
ice, to serve
juicer
SERVES 2

Kiwis are my secret weapon against colds, being rich in vitamin C. They are sharp and sweet, and mixed with the mellower flavours of pears and apples they make a really gorgeous early-morning juice.

Pass the pears, kiwis and apples through
a juicer, one at a time, into a jug. Add
enough ice for 2 people and serve.

Basil limeade

225 ml/1 scant cup lime
    juice (from about
    10 limes)
75 g/⅓ cup packed light
    brown sugar
a handful of fresh basil
    leaves
2 handfuls of ice
250 ml/1 cup soda water
*4–6 cocktail glasses, chilled
    in the freezer for 1 hour*
SERVES 4–6

If I'm having a brunch gathering then this basil limeade is what I serve to guests. The amount of lime and sugar is a personal thing, so I suggest you adjust it to taste, adding more of one or the other as necessary. There will be guests who will appreciate a cheeky dash of cachaça rum in theirs for a caipirinha-style cocktail.

Put the lime juice, sugar and basil in a blender (one that is able to crush ice) and blend until smooth. Add the ice and blend briefly to break up the ice cubes. Pour into the cocktail glasses and top up with the soda water.

Basil limeade (right)

Pineapple & mint agua fresca

100 g/½ cup granulated
    sugar
a smallish pineapple (about
    700 g/1¾ lbs.), peeled
    and cored
a small handful of fresh
    mint leaves, plus extra
    to serve
ice, to serve
600 ml/2⅓ cups chilled
    soda water (optional)
SERVES 4–8

Refreshing *agua fresca* is found all over Mexico. The name literally means 'cold water' and it can be any fruit (or even another ingredient such as tamarind or rice and milk) blended with ice, sugar and water. The idea is that it is cooling and rehydrating on a hot day. Serve it as a whipped fruit frappé just with ice, or as a sparkling drink mixed with soda water.

Put the sugar and 100 ml/½ cup water in a saucepan and heat gently until the sugar has dissolved. Remove from the heat and let cool while you cut the pineapple into rough chunks. Put the pineapple in a blender with the mint and the cooled syrup. Blend until smooth. Divide between 4 tumblers with a scoop of ice in each one, or 8 tall glasses and top up with ice and the soda water.

Pomegranate & orange sunrise

ice, to serve
500 ml/2 cups freshly
    squeezed orange juice
200 ml/¾ cup pure
    pomegranate juice
SERVES 2

A twist on the usual tequila sunrise, mine is made with the newly fashionable pomegranate juice which adds a twist of bitterness to cut through the natural sweetness of orange juice. I sometimes add a shot of Campari to the pomegranate juice too, but this makes it an entirely different kind of morning!

Half fill 2 tumblers with ice and top up with orange juice so they are two-thirds full. Pour the pomegranate juice slowly down the side of the glass so it sinks to the bottom. Serve straightaway with a cocktail stirrer.

Banana, honey & wheatgerm lassi

2 bananas, peeled
2 teaspoons clear honey
100 g/½ cup plain yogurt
150 ml/⅔ cup whole milk
1 tablespoon wheatgerm
 or wheat bran
SERVES 2

Some mornings I need a smoothie which is a meal in itself, especially if I am awake early and can't face eating. With the added bite of the wheatgerm, this lassi fits the bill. Lassi is a cooling Indian drink which can be sweet or savoury. In the summer I add a handful of ice before blending it for a more chilled drink. If you like ripe bananas, let the skins become speckled for a more intense experience.

Put the bananas, honey, yogurt and milk in a blender and blend until smooth. Taste and add a little more honey if you think it needs it. Stir in the wheatgerm and blend briefly just to mix. Divide between 2 tall glasses and serve with straws big enough for the wheatgerm not to cause blockages.

Cashew nut & mango smoothie

50 g/⅓ cup shelled cashew
 nuts, soaked overnight in
 cold water
1 ripe mango, peeled, pitted
 and roughly chopped
1 teaspoon linseed
SERVES 2

It's easy to forget how milky blended cashew nuts are, but they do make brilliant dairy-free smoothies. I like to blend mine with mango as it results in a super-thick smoothie verging on dessert territory. You could also use soft berries or bananas.

Drain the cashew nuts and put in a blender with 150 ml/⅔ cup water. Blend until you have a smooth, nutty milk. Add the chopped mango. Blend again, then stir in the linseed. Divide between 2 tumblers and serve.

Raspberry, strawberry & orange juice

125 g/1 cup frozen
 raspberries
125 g/1 cup strawberries,
 hulled
400 ml/1⅔ cups freshly
 squeezed orange juice
SERVES 2–4

I like to keep raspberries in my freezer for a rainy day as they add body to smoothies as well as a sharp burst of fruity flavour. There's no need to add ice, as the raspberries will make the drink lovely and icy for you.

Put the raspberries, strawberries and orange juice in a blender and blend until smooth. Divide between 2–4 tumblers and serve.

Raspberry, strawberry & orange juice; Banana, honey & wheatgerm lassi; and Cashew nut & mango smoothie (left to right)

Bloody mary

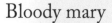

150 ml/²⁄₃ cup vodka

450 ml/1²⁄₃ cups pure
   tomato juice

½ teaspoon hot
   horseradish sauce

1 teaspoon Worcestershire
   sauce

4 dashes Tabasco sauce

¼ teaspoon celery salt

½ teaspoon cracked
   black pepper

2 limes, cut into small
   wedges

ice, to serve

SERVES 4

There's nothing like a good Bloody Mary after a late night: it seems to get the blood pumping and cure any feelings of drowsiness. If you want a Virgin Mary leave out the vodka but squeeze in some more lime so you get more of a tang in it.

Mix all the ingredients together in a jug. Taste and adjust the seasonings if necessary, adding more heat, pepper or lime as you wish. Add a couple of handfuls of ice and serve with a stack of tumblers.

Sea breeze

This is a great morning drink for summer. Simple to make and really refreshing but a few glasses will make you feel pleasantly sleepy, so watch you don't end up crawling back into bed.

a handful of ice
150 ml/²⁄₃ cup pure pink
   grapefruit juice
300 ml/1¹⁄₃ cups pure
   cranberry juice
100 ml/½ cup vodka
1 lime, cut into wedges
cocktail shaker
SERVES 2

Put the ice in the cocktail shaker along with the juices and vodka. Squeeze over a couple of lime wedges. Put the top on the shaker and shake a few times. Strain into 2 tall glasses and add a lime wedge to each before serving.

Blood orange & campari mimosa

Mimosa or Buck's Fizz is a standard offering at brunch gatherings, but this one is different. The Campari and blood orange make it a little bitter, and this really whets the appetite. If anyone needs his or hers sweetened – not everyone gets the bitter thing – add a dash of agave syrup or honey and serve with a cocktail stirrer.

500 ml/2 cups pure blood
   orange juice
2 tablespoons Campari
750-ml bottle sparkling
   white wine, chilled
SERVES 4

Divide the blood orange juice between 4 champagne flutes. Add a dash of Campari to each one, then top up with the wine.

Blood orange & campari mimosa (above)

Lemon & sage tisane

a small handful of fresh
  sage leaves
1 lemon
600 ml/2½ cups boiling
  water
1–2 teaspoons honey,
  to taste
SERVES 2

A tisane is a herbal tea, made strictly without real tea. Instead it is made by infusing herbs, spices or any aromatics in hot water. My lemony tisane infused with sage is a great drink for the morning – it will brighten your eyes and leave your face with a warm glow, if nothing else.

Put the sage leaves in a teapot. Using a potato peeler, pare off the lemon zest leaving behind the white pith underneath. Add this to the teapot. Halve the slightly naked-looking lemon and squeeze out all its juice, then set aside. Pour the boiling water over the leaves and zest and let steep for 3–5 minutes, depending on how strong you like it. Pour into 2 mugs and add lemon juice and honey to taste.

Real hot chocolate

500 ml/2 cups whole milk
1 vanilla pod/bean, split
  lengthways
75 g/3½ oz. dark
  chocolate (at least 70%
  cocoa solids), coarsely
  grated, plus extra to dust
1 tablespoon light brown
  sugar
SERVES 2

Once you have had proper hot chocolate there is no going back I'm afraid. Pick a really good cooking chocolate with at least 70% cocoa solids to make this, so that you get a really chocolatey flavour.

Pour the milk into a saucepan and add the vanilla pod/bean. Slowly bring to a gentle simmer, then remove from the heat and set aside for 10 minutes to allow the flavour to infuse the milk. Add the chocolate and sugar and whisk into the milk until melted and dissolved. Return to a low heat until steaming, but not boiling. Remove the vanilla pod/bean, then divide between 2 mugs. Dust with chocolate.

Spiced mocha

300 ml/1¼ cups whole milk
1 cinnamon stick
a pinch of grated nutmeg
2 shots of espresso coffee
2 tablespoons cocoa
  powder
1–2 tablespoons demerara
  sugar
100 ml/½ cup whipping
  cream, whipped to soft
  peaks
SERVES 2

I find coffee to be quite bitter but I love hot chocolate, so for me, this is the best of both worlds: the hit of caffeine with the luxurious sweetness of a good steaming mug of cocoa. The spices give it a real complexity and stop it becoming sickly sweet. I can't justify the whipped cream on top, but I think it would be foolish to make it without.

Pour the milk into a saucepan and add the cinnamon and nutmeg. Slowly bring to a gentle simmer, then remove from the heat and set aside for 10 minutes to allow the flavours to infuse the milk. Meanwhile, pour the espresso shots into a heatproof jug. Stir in the cocoa powder and sugar until blended. Add the hot milk and whisk until all the ingredients are well blended. Return to the pan and reheat gently. Divide between 2 mugs and top with whipped cream.

fruit, grains & oats

Strawberries with pine nuts & greek yogurt Melon salad in stem ginger syrup **Poached pears in jasmine tea syrup with cinnamon & dates** Rhubarb & orange compote Pink grapefruit with vanilla sugar **Bircher muesli** Toasted coconut & tropical fruit muesli Nutty honey granola **Porridge with apples & blackberries** Deep coconut & sour cherry oaty bars Apricot & pumpkin seed granola bars **Irish oatmeal with bananas, maple syrup & pecans** Granola, nectarine & ricotta parfait

Strawberries with pine nuts & greek yogurt

450 g/3 cups strawberries, hulled and halved

2 tablespoons golden granulated/natural cane sugar

3 tablespoons dark brown sugar

250 g/1 cup Greek yogurt

3 tablespoons pine nuts

SERVES 4

When strawberries are at their most fragrant, with their candy floss perfume, this is the perfect breakfast dish to whip up. Crumbling dark brown sugar over the voluptuous Greek yogurt creates a pool of fudginess on top. All the treacly flavours which come from the natural molasses in the sugar are drawn out; these contrast beautifully against the yogurt and enhance the sweet berries.

Put the strawberries in a bowl and scatter over the granulated/natural cane sugar. Cover and let macerate for 10 minutes. Scatter the dark brown sugar over the yogurt in a separate bowl and set aside.

Meanwhile, put the pine nuts in a heavy-based frying pan over low heat and toast for 2–3 minutes, shaking them about until they become golden on all sides.

Divide the strawberries between 4 bowls. Swirl the now fudgy dark brown sugar through the yogurt and spoon on top of the strawberries. Scatter the pine nuts on top and serve.

Melon salad in stem ginger syrup

100 g/½ cup light brown sugar

50 g/2 oz. stem ginger, drained and finely chopped

juice of 1 lemon

1 charentais or Cantaloupe melon, peeled and deseeded

200 g/1¼ cups raspberries (optional)

SERVES 4

Ginger and melon are quite simply a match made in culinary heaven. The sweetness of one sets off the sharpness of the other one and vice versa. Make this when melons are bursting with ripe perfume and the raspberries, if you'd like to use some, are as sweet as can be.

Put the light brown sugar in a saucepan with the ginger and 200 ml/¾ cup water. Heat gently until the sugar has completely dissolved, then turn up the heat and simmer for 5 minutes. Remove from the heat and add the lemon juice. Let cool.

Slice or chop the melon, place in a bowl and pour over the syrup. Tumble over the raspberries, if using, then serve.

Poached pears in jasmine tea syrup with cinnamon & dates

200 ml/¾ cup boiling water

1 tablespoon jasmine tea leaves

2 cinnamon sticks

75 g/⅓ cup (clear) honey

4 small pears, peeled, halved and cored

225 g/1½ cups Medjool dates, pitted and sliced

plain yogurt or ricotta, to serve

SERVES 4

I love using tea leaves to imbue syrups with a delicate flavour. Jasmine tea is one of the most fragrant flavours, especially if you look out for the high-quality teas whose leaves are furled into long shapes.

Let the boiling water cool for a few minutes so it doesn't scorch the delicate tea leaves. Once it has cooled slightly – ideally 90°C/195°F, but don't worry, you don't need to check with a thermometer – you can pour it onto the jasmine tea leaves in a teapot or a heatproof jug/pitcher. Let it steep for 3 minutes.

Strain the jasmine tea into a saucepan. Add the cinnamon and honey and place over medium heat. Bring it to a gentle simmer, then lower in the pears.

Cut out a disk of greaseproof paper to fit inside the pan, scrunch it up, then open it out again. Lower it into the pan and cover with the lid. Simmer gently for 8 minutes, then turn the pears so the other side sees the syrup (replacing the paper disk and lid). Simmer for 8 minutes. Add the dates and simmer for 5 minutes (still with the paper disk and lid on). Remove from the heat and let stand for 10 minutes. Serve warm or cold with plain yogurt or ricotta.

Rhubarb & orange compote

Add blueberries or strawberries to this basic cushion of pink rhubarb. Keep your eye out for bright pink forced rhubarb, which is grown indoors in the dark for its lurid colour, making it an uplifting winter treat.

400 g/14 oz. rhubarb

grated zest of ½ orange

juice of 1 orange

1 vanilla pod/bean, split
   lengthways

150 g/¾ cup light brown
   sugar

plain yogurt or porridge/
   hot cereal, to serve

SERVES 4

Preheat the oven to 180°C (350°F) Gas 4.

Trim the rhubarb to remove any leaves and the tough ends and cut into 7-cm/3-inch lengths. Put these stubby bits of rhubarb, along with the orange zest, juice and vanilla pod/bean in a large baking dish and scatter the sugar over the top.

Cover the dish with foil and roast in the preheated oven for 15–20 minutes, until the rhubarb compliantly softens up.

Let cool and serve with a generous dollop of yogurt or a bowl of steaming porridge, or simply by itself. Store in the fridge for up to 1 week.

Pink grapefruit with vanilla sugar

2 pink grapefruits

1 vanilla pod/bean, split lengthways

2 tablespoons (golden caster) sugar

plain yogurt, to serve (optional)

SERVES 4

This is a quick and easy way to serve zingy grapefruit. If you happen to have one of those snazzy curved grapefruit knives, now is the moment you have been waiting for. You really do need to loosen the flesh from the shell before you grill/broil it, as a hot grapefruit becomes quite dangerous when you try to delve into it with a spoon. Don't fret if you don't have a grapefruit knife – a small paring knife does a good job too.

Halve the grapefruits and slice a little off each top and bottom so they sit securely on a flat surface. Loosen the flesh from the shell with a curved grapefruit knife or small paring knife.

Scrape the seeds out of the vanilla pod/bean and add to the sugar. Mix thoroughly with the back of a spoon to spread out the seeds.

Preheat the grill/broiler.

Place each grapefruit half on a baking sheet and sprinkle the sugar over them. Slide under the grill/broiler and let the sugar melt and caramelize. It should only take 2–3 minutes. Remove from under the grill/broiler and let cool for 2 minutes. Serve with plain yogurt on the side or if you are being abstemious, by itself.

Bircher muesli

125 g/1 cup rolled oats

75 g/½ cup (golden) raisins

175 ml/¾ cup apple juice

juice of 1 lemon

100 g/¼ cup plain yogurt

1 apple, cored, peeled and grated

3 tablespoons flaked/slivered almonds

mixed summer berries, to serve

honey, to serve

SERVES 4–6

This is what I like to call summer porridge. It has the type of texture you either love or hate. I adore it – there is something comforting about its soggy sweetness – but my husband prefers crunchy granola. Each to his own. It will keep for 2–3 days in the fridge, but in that case, leave the apple out so it doesn't brown.

Put the oats and raisins in a large dish. Pour over the apple and lemon juices. Cover with a dish cloth and let soak overnight. Alternatively place in an airtight container and refrigerate, especially if it is very hot.

The next morning when you're ready for breakfast, stir the yogurt, apple and almonds into the soaked muesli. Divide between 4–6 bowls, scatter some brightly coloured berries over the top and finish with a zigzag of (clear) honey.

Bircher muesli (right)

Toasted coconut & tropical fruit muesli

300 g/2⅓ cups rolled oats
50 g/⅓ cup black (or
   white) sesame seeds
50 g/⅓ cup sunflower seeds
125 ml/½ cup apple juice
3 tablespoons vegetable oil
50 g/⅓ cup desiccated
   coconut
50 g/⅓ cup dried mango,
   finely chopped
50 g/⅓ cup dried
   pineapple, finely chopped
50 g/⅓ cup dried papaya,
   finely chopped
1–2 large baking sheets,
   lined with baking
   parchment
SERVES 6–8

This toasted muesli is made with apple juice instead of being coated in sugar or honey, as most granola is. It crisps up the oats, but isn't overly sweet. I like the chewy tanginess of tropical fruits, but any dried fruits will work as they are simply stirred in at the end. If you can find some black sesame seeds, often sold in Asian grocers, they stand out more, but the regular ones are fine too.

Preheat the oven to 150°C (300°F) Gas 2.

Pour the oats and seeds into a really large mixing bowl, then stir in the apple juice and oil. Toss well until the juice has soaked into the dry ingredients. Tip half of the mixture onto each prepared baking sheet and spread out evenly. Bake in the preheated oven for 25 minutes, until the oats are starting to toast.

Remove the baking sheets from the oven and give everything a good stir. Add the desiccated coconut to the oat mixture and bake for a further 20 minutes. Let cool completely.

When the muesli is cold, stir in all the chopped dried fruit and toss to distribute evenly. Store in an airtight container and eat within 3 weeks.

Nutty honey granola

125 g/½ cup maple syrup
125 g/½ cup (clear) honey
4 tablespoons sunflower oil
250 g/2 cups rolled oats
75 g/⅔ cup shelled
   almonds, roughly
   chopped
75 g/⅔ cup shelled Brazil
   nuts, roughly chopped
50 g/⅓ cup pumpkin seeds
½ teaspoon salt
100 g/⅔ cup (golden)
   raisins
1–2 large baking sheets,
   lined with baking
   parchment
SERVES 10–12

Mmmm, crunchy honeyed granola. This version is very sweet and crunchy and quite rich so you don't need a lot. I tend to have a scattering with my yogurt rather than the other way round. The trick is to get it to brown evenly, so you need it to be spread out and to turn it during roasting. Don't let it become too dark or it gets bitter. If in doubt, take it out and let it cool a little, then taste it and you can always put it back in for longer.

Preheat the oven to 140°C (275°F) Gas 1.

Put the maple syrup, honey and oil in a small saucepan and set over low heat to warm through. Put the oats, nuts, seeds and salt in a large mixing bowl and stir well. Pour over the warmed syrup and mix thoroughly with a wooden spoon. All the oats must be moistened.

Spread the granola over the prepared baking sheets, making sure it is no deeper than 1 cm/½ inch, and bake in the preheated oven for 20 minutes.

Remove the sheets from the oven and stir the toasted, golden granola from the edges to the middle, then smooth out again. Return to the oven for a further 15–20 minutes, until lightly golden. Don't expect it to become crunchy – the mixture will remain soft until it cools.

Remove from the oven and let cool for 10 minutes before stirring in the raisins. Let cool completely, then break into pieces. Store in an airtight container and eat within 1 month.

Nutty honey granola (left)

Porridge with apples & blackberries

100 g/¾ cup rolled oats

250 ml/1 cup whole milk,
plus a little extra to thin

a pinch of salt

75 g/½ cup (golden) raisins

1 tablespoon butter

2 apples, cored and cut
into slim wedges

3 tablespoons demerara
sugar

a pinch of ground
cinnamon

100 g/1 cup blackberries

SERVES 4

Everyone likes their porridge prepared differently. Personally I find porridge made with all milk too cloying and when it's made with just water a little insipid, unless you add a swirl of cream at the end which rather defeats the purpose of using good old water. A pinch of salt is a must too, as this stops it from being flabby and gives it some backbone.

Put the oats in a saucepan and add the milk and 250 ml/1 cup water. Add a pinch of salt, cover with a lid and slowly bring to the boil over medium heat. Once the mixture is bubbling, turn the heat to low, add the raisins and cook for 2–3 minutes, stirring occasionally. The porridge should be thick and creamy. Take off the heat and let stand with a lid on for 2–3 minutes while you cook the apples.

Put the butter in a frying pan over high heat until the bubbling subsides.

Stir in the apples, sugar and cinnamon. Let caramelize for 2–3 minutes, then flip the apple wedges over so the other side gets a chance to become golden too. Finally, add the blackberries and heat for a couple of minutes just so they warm through a little.

Meanwhile, spoon the porridge into 4 bowls and stir in a little cold milk to stop it becoming too thick. Spoon the caramelized apples and blackberries on top and serve straightaway.

Deep coconut & sour cherry oaty bars

100 g/²⁄₃ cup dried sour cherries

100 g/6½ tablespoons unsalted butter, cubed

125 g/½ cup golden syrup

175 g/¾ cup light brown sugar

½ teaspoon ground cinnamon

75 g/½ cup desiccated coconut

225 g/1¾ cups rolled oats

75 g/generous ½ cup self-raising flour

½ teaspoon bicarbonate of/baking soda

a pinch of salt

20 x 20-cm/8 x 8-in. baking pan, lined with parchment

MAKES 9

These oat bars flecked with dried cherries are chewy and moist. The butter and syrupy sweetness in them are usually reserved for an indulgent teatime treat, but they also go down very well in the morning.

Preheat the oven to 180°C (350°F) Gas 4.

Put the cherries in a bowl of boiling water and let soak for 10 minutes.

Meanwhile, put the butter, golden syrup and sugar in a saucepan and heat gently until dissolved and melted. Stir in the cinnamon. Pour the coconut, oats, flour, bicarbonate of/baking soda and salt over the butter mixture and stir to combine. Drain the cherries and add those. Once everything is well mixed, pack the mixture into the prepared baking pan, pressing it down with a palette knife to compact it. Bake in the preheated oven for 25–30 minutes, until golden at the sides.

Remove from the oven and let cool for 10 minutes. Turn the mixture out onto a board and cut into 9 squares. Let cool, then store in an airtight container and eat within 5 days.

Apricot & pumpkin seed granola bars

225 g/1¾ cups rolled oats

100 g/²⁄₃ cup pumpkin seeds

50 g/⅓ cup wheatgerm or wheat bran

½ teaspoon ground ginger

½ teaspoon salt

85 g/²⁄₃ cup dried apricots, chopped

150 g/²⁄₃ cup honey

50 g/¼ cup light brown sugar

6 tablespoons sunflower oil

20 x 30-cm/8 x 12-in. baking pan, lined with parchment

MAKES 14

In the name of good health, I have come up with a crunchier, snappier, less buttery bar than those above. They are not chewy but they will hit the spot in the morning. You can vary the dried fruit and spice as much as you like as long as you stick to the basic premise.

Preheat the oven to 180°C (350°F) Gas 4.

Put the oats, pumpkin seeds, wheatgerm, ginger, salt and apricots in a large mixing bowl. Put the honey, sugar and oil in a saucepan over low heat. Heat for 4–5 minutes, until the sugar has melted into the butter.

Remove from the heat and pour the melted mixture over the dry ingredients in the mixing bowl, stirring so the mixture moistens all over. Spoon the mixture into the prepared baking pan and smooth it out with a palette knife. Bake in the preheated oven for 20–22 minutes, until golden around the edges.

Remove from the oven and let cool for 10 minutes. Turn the mixture out onto a board and cut into 14 bars. Let cool, then store in an airtight container and eat within 5 days.

Apricot & pumpkin seed granola bars, and Deep coconut & sour cherry oaty bars (left to right)

Irish oatmeal with bananas, maple syrup & pecans

175 g/1¼ cups Irish or
steel-cut oats
a pinch of salt
50 g/⅓ cup shelled pecans,
chopped
3 tablespoons double/
heavy cream
2 bananas, sliced
pure maple syrup, to serve
SERVES 4–6

For proper oatmeal you will need to buy oats that haven't been rolled. These are called Irish, steel-cut or pinhead oats and are coarser than rolled oats. This means a lot of extra cooking, which in turn means you need to reorganize yourself and put the oats on before you feed your cats, shower etc., and then you won't have to wait for them. The result is a much more al dente mass of oaty nuggets in a creamy risotto-like sauce. They also need quite a generous pinch of salt.

Heat 1.2 litres/5 cups water in a heavy-based saucepan until it comes to the boil, then tip in the oats and salt. Cover with a lid and turn the heat down as low as possible so there is no danger of sticking.

Put the pecans in a dry frying pan over medium heat and let them heat up. Stir so they brown evenly, then remove from the heat and set aside.

Go off and have your shower or walk the dog and, after 30 minutes, the oats will be ready. Check they are not sticking after about 20 minutes, the first time you cook them. After that you will have it all sussed out.

Stir in the cream, then spoon into bowls and scatter over the bananas and pecans. Serve with maple syrup.

Granola, nectarine & ricotta parfait

150 g/⅔ cup plain sheep's
yogurt
250 g/1 cup ricotta
300 g/2 cups Nutty Honey
Granola (page 33)
4 nectarines, pitted and
sliced
100 g/⅔ cup raspberries
4 tablespoons/¼ cup
(clear) honey, plus extra
to drizzle
SERVES 4

These little pots of deliciousness are perfect to offer guests at a brunch party as an alternative to the fat-laden fry-up. Layer the ricotta, fruit and granola in glasses for a groovy look. You can vary the fruit depending on the season, but if you use hard fruits, such as apples or pears, poach them in some sugar syrup first until they are as soft as a ripe nectarine.

Put the yogurt and ricotta in a bowl and beat together until combined.

Divide half the granola between 4 glasses, then put some nectarine slices and raspberries on top of that. Top with some of the yogurt mixture and honey.

Top with the remaining granola, followed by more nectarines and raspberries, saving a few for the top, and another spoonful or two of the yogurt mixture. Arrange the remaining fruit on top, drizzle with more honey and serve straightaway.

Granola, nectarine & ricotta parfait (right)

eggs

Eggs benedict Fried eggs with sage pangritata, asparagus & pancetta **Herb fritters with fried eggs & sumac tomatoes** Poached eggs on spinach with yogurt & spiced butter Eggs en cocotte with leeks & tapenade **Scrambled eggs with smoked trout & shiso** Huevos rancheros Soft-boiled eggs with prosciutto-wrapped focaccia **Caramelized chicory/belgian endive with black forest ham & poached eggs** French toast with provolone & half-dried tomatoes Omelette with chives & gruyère **Smoked haddock, radish & avocado omelette wraps** Tortilla with potatoes, chillies & peppers Wild mushroom mini-frittatas with garlic sourdough croutons

Eggs benedict

4 large eggs

2 whole-grain muffins, halved horizontally

8 slices of thin-cut ham

freshly ground black pepper

HOLLANDAISE SAUCE

2 tablespoons white wine vinegar

1 shallot, roughly chopped

½ teaspoon black peppercorns

2 large egg yolks

120 g/1 stick unsalted butter

SERVES 4

This dish is all about timing. Get everything ready before you cook the eggs and you won't have to rush. Hollandaise sauce made in a blender is easy – just add the butter very slowly and you should hear the sauce turning thick and slushy.

Preheat the grill/broiler.

To make the hollandaise sauce, put the vinegar, 2 tablespoons cold water, the shallot and peppercorns in a saucepan and simmer over low heat for a few minutes until you have 1 tablespoon liquid remaining. Strain into a blender (or in a bowl if you are going to use an electric handheld whisk) with the egg yolks and set aside. Melt the butter in the same pan.

Fill a large, deep frying pan with water and bring to a simmer. Crack the eggs around the edge so they don't touch and poach for exactly 3 minutes. Meanwhile,

put the muffins (cut side up) and ham on a baking sheet. Grill/broil for 2–3 minutes.

To finish the sauce, blend the eggs and vinegar until frothy. With the motor still running, add the melted butter in a very slow trickle until the sauce is thick. You should take about a minute to add all the butter. Any quicker and it will not emulsify and you'll be left with runny eggs.

Drape 2 slices of ham on top of each muffin half. Scoop out each poached egg and add to the stack. Pour over the hollandaise sauce and sprinkle with a grinding of black pepper.

Fried eggs with sage pangritata, asparagus & pancetta

2 slices of sourdough bread, torn into chunks, crust and all

5 tablespoons olive oil

10 fresh sage leaves, shredded

400 g/14 oz. asparagus, trimmed

100 g/3½ oz. pancetta, cubed

4 large eggs

sea salt and freshly ground black pepper

SERVES 4

Roasting asparagus is my favourite way of cooking it: the flavour is intensified and the ends get frazzled. Pangritata – fried breadcrumbs with herbs – was devised by the Italians to provide a similar texture and flavour to Parmesan, but cheaply.

Preheat the oven to 190°C (375°F) Gas 5.

Whizz the bread in a food processor until you get chunky, uneven crumbs. Tip out onto a baking sheet and drizzle over 2 tablespoons of the oil, the sage and some seasoning. Toss everything together, then bake in the preheated oven for 15 minutes, stirring a couple of times to ensure it browns evenly.

Snap off the pale, woody ends of the asparagus and discard. Put the stems on a baking sheet, drizzle with 2 tablespoons of the oil and season. Toss, then scatter

the pancetta over the top. Roast in the oven for 10–12 minutes, until the pancetta is cooked through and the asparagus is tender and slightly frazzled.

Heat the remaining oil in a frying pan over high heat, then crack an egg in each corner and turn the heat right down. Cook for 2–3 minutes until the white has set. If you need to firm up the white, cover with the lid for 30 seconds.

Divide the asparagus between 4 plates, top with an egg and sprinkle the pangritata over the top.

Eggs benedict (right)

Herb fritters with fried eggs & sumac tomatoes

4 or 5 plum tomatoes,
    roughly chopped

2 teaspoons ground sumac

3 tablespoons extra virgin
    olive oil, or more

5 large eggs

1 teaspoon ground cumin

2 big handfuls of fresh
    flat-leaf parsley, leaves
    roughly chopped and
    stalks discarded

1 small handful of fresh
    coriander/cilantro, leaves
    roughly chopped and
    stalks discarded

sea salt and freshly ground
    black pepper

SERVES 4

Sumac is a wild berry which, when dried and ground, adds a sour tang to food, a little like lemon juice. These herb fritters are a good way of using up leaves from a bush of herbs that needs trimming back. Serve it for a low-carb brekkie.

Preheat the oven to low.

Put the tomatoes and sumac in a bowl with 1 tablespoon of the oil. Season and toss until coated, then set aside.

Crack one of the eggs into a mixing bowl, season, add the cumin and beat to mix. Stir in the herbs. It will look like there is not enough egg, but you only need enough to bind it.

Heat a frying pan over high heat and add 1 tablespoon of the oil. Drop 2 tablespoons of the herb mixture in the pan to make your first fritter and continue until you run out of space in the pan. Cook over high heat for 2 minutes on each side, until lightly golden. Keep warm in the oven while you fry the rest.

Once all the fritters are done, add the remaining oil to the same frying pan and wait for it to heat up. Crack the remaining eggs into the pan and fry for 2 minutes. Cover with a lid and cook for a further 30–40 seconds just to cook the top of the whites; you want the egg yolk to remain runny.

Divide the fritters between 4 plates, top with a fried egg and scatter the sumac tomatoes over the top.

Poached eggs on spinach with yogurt & spiced butter

1 small garlic clove, crushed

200 g/¾ cup Greek yogurt

50 g/3 tablespoons butter

½ teaspoon cumin seeds

½ teaspoon dried chilli/hot
    pepper flakes

½ teaspoon sea salt flakes

1 loaf of Turkish flat bread,
    cut into 4 squares and
    halved horizontally

1 tablespoon olive oil

400 g/14 oz. spinach

8 large eggs

sea salt and freshly ground
    black pepper

SERVES 4

This egg dish is packed with so much flavour that you will be hooked from the first taste. If you can't get hold of Turkish bread then pita or sourdough work well.

Preheat the grill/broiler to high. Get everything ready before you start cooking: mix the garlic and yogurt. Put the butter, cumin, chilli/pepper flakes and salt flakes in a small saucepan. Put the flat bread on a baking sheet. Fill 2 deep frying pans with water and bring to the boil over high heat.

Heat a wok, then add the oil and when hot, add the spinach in batches. Toss around the wok so it cooks evenly and when it is just wilted, take it off the heat, season and cover.

Reduce the heat under the 2 frying pans to low so the water is barely simmering and break 4 eggs, far apart, into each pan. Leave for 3 minutes. Grill/broil the bread, cut side up, until lightly toasted, then transfer to 4 plates. Spread some garlic yogurt over the bread and heap a mound of spinach on top. Using a slotted spoon, sit a poached egg on top of each square of yogurty bread. Quickly heat the spiced butter over high heat until bubbling, pour over the eggs and serve.

Poached eggs on spinach with yogurt & spiced butter (left)

Eggs en cocotte with leeks & tapenade

25 g/2 tablespoons butter

2 leeks, thinly sliced

a pinch of ground nutmeg

2 tablespoons tapenade
(olive paste)

4 large eggs

2 tablespoons double/
heavy cream

sea salt and freshly ground
black pepper

whole-grain toast or green
salad, to serve

4 x 150-ml/5-oz. ramekins

SERVES 4

Eggs *en cocotte* – baked eggs – are all about timing: you want that yolk to have a good molten ooze. Don't skip the *bain marie* part otherwise the whites will become overheated and tough. If you like you can put some chopped sautéed mushrooms or pesto in the base of the ramekins. Sometimes I buy porcini and truffle paste from a deli and use that, as it has such a natural affinity with eggs.

Preheat the oven to 200°C (400°F) Gas 6.

Heat the butter in a frying pan, add the leeks and cook gently for 5–6 minutes until soft. Season to taste with salt, pepper and nutmeg.

Spoon an equal amount of tapenade into each ramekin, then top with the leeks. Break an egg into each ramekin, season them too, then drizzle a trickle of the cream over the top of each.

Put the ramekins in a deep roasting pan in the oven and pour enough boiling water directly from the kettle into the roasting pan so that it comes about halfway up the sides of the ramekins. This is the *bain marie*. Bake in the preheated oven for 10–14 minutes – 10 minutes if you like the yolks to remain runny, and a few minutes more if you prefer them set.

Lift the ramekins carefully out of the roasting pan using tongs and serve straightaway as they will continue to cook. Serve with whole-grain toast or green salad on the side.

Scrambled eggs with smoked trout & shiso

10 large eggs

4 tablespoons whole milk

50 g/3 tablespoons butter

4 slices of white bread

280 g/9 oz. smoked trout,
flaked

a handful of shiso cress or
radish sprouts

a pinch of Japanese chilli
(hot) pepper or chilli
powder/ground red chile

sea salt and freshly ground
black pepper

SERVES 4

Scrambled eggs need to be cooked with patience to become creamy. If they are cooked properly, you will not have to resort to adding cream, which just hides an underlying bad scramble. Smoked trout goes exceedingly well with scrambled eggs and the pretty purple leaves of shiso cress decorate it and add a spicy kick.

Break the eggs into a mixing bowl and beat together with the milk and some salt and pepper.

Meanwhile, heat half the butter in a heavy-based saucepan over low heat until the bubbling subsides. Pour in the eggs and heat through, stirring occasionally, for 4–5 minutes, until they start to feel like they are in danger of catching on the base of the pan. Reduce the heat to its lowest setting and stir constantly for 3–5 minutes to make sure the eggs are not over-heating on the bottom of the pan.

Meanwhile, toast and butter the bread with the remaining butter. Take the eggs off the heat while they still look a little runny, add the trout, give them a final few stirs and divide between the pieces of toast. Scatter the shiso and a little chilli pepper over the top.

Scrambled eggs with smoked trout & shiso (right)

Huevos rancheros

3 tablespoons vegetable oil

1 green chilli or jalapeño pepper, chopped

2 garlic cloves, crushed

500 g/1 lb. tomatoes, cut into slim wedges

400-g/14-oz. can pinto or cannellini beans

50 g/½ cup grated sharp cheddar

juice of 1 lime, plus extra lime wedges to serve

a handful of fresh coriander/cilantro leaves, chopped

4 eggs

4 corn tortillas

sea salt and freshly ground black pepper

SERVES 4

I like to cook my salsa with fresh tomatoes and then serve it with mashed, cheesy beans and these huevos rancheros. You can buy cans of refried beans but it is just as easy to mash your own. If you want to serve it with a spoonful of guacamole or sour cream, that's a great idea.

Heat 1 tablespoon of the oil in a large frying pan over medium heat, then add the chilli, half the garlic and a pinch of salt and fry for 1–2 minutes, until softened. Add the tomatoes and cook gently for about 20 minutes.

Heat the remaining oil in a small saucepan, add the remaining garlic and heat through for 20 seconds, until just browning. Add the beans, then using a potato masher, coarsely mash the beans and stir in plenty of salt and pepper and the cheddar.

Stir the lime juice and coriander/cilantro into the tomato sauce. Make 4 holes in the sauce and crack an egg into each one. Cook for 3 minutes until set. Cover with the lid for the last 30 seconds just to firm up the whites.

Meanwhile, heat a frying pan over medium heat. Cook the tortillas for 1 minute on each side, until golden and hot. Transfer to 4 plates and spread the beans over the tortillas. Top with tomato salsa and the eggs. Serve with lime wedges and guacamole or sour cream if you like.

Soft-boiled eggs with prosciutto-wrapped focaccia

1 teaspoon anchovy paste

3 tablespoons extra virgin olive oil

8 x 1-cm/½-in. slices of rosemary focaccia, halved horizontally

4 large eggs, at room temperature

8 slices of prosciutto, each torn in half

SERVES 4

The method below is by far the best for soft-boiling eggs. In fact, the word 'boiled' is misleading because boiling an egg toughens up the white, making it rubbery, not creamy. The timings here will give you a perfectly runny yolk with a set, creamy white. This will only work if the eggs are at room temperature to start with – don't cook them straight out of the fridge otherwise they will crack.

Preheat the grill/broiler.

Mix the anchovy paste with the oil and spread it over the focaccia. Bring a medium saucepan of water to a rolling boil. Lower in the eggs and turn the heat down so they simmer gently for 1 minute. Turn off the heat completely, cover with a lid and set your timer for 4 minutes.

Meanwhile, grill/broil the focaccia, anchovy side up, for 1–2 minutes. Remove from the grill/broiler and wrap a piece of prosciutto around each toast. Place on a plate with an egg cup. Remove the eggs from the water with a slotted spoon and transfer to the egg cups. Eat immediately otherwise the eggs will continue to cook.

Huevos rancheros (left)

Caramelized chicory/belgian endive with black forest ham & poached eggs

25 g/2 tablespoons butter

4 chicory/Belgian endive
heads, halved lengthways

4 eggs

100 g/3½ oz. rocket/arugula

8 slices of Black Forest ham

25 g/1 oz. Parmesan, shaved

sea salt and freshly ground
black pepper

DRESSING

1 small garlic clove,
finely chopped

1 red chilli, finely chopped

1 tablespoon red wine
vinegar

2 tablespoons extra virgin
olive oil

finely grated zest and juice
of ½ unwaxed lemon

SERVES 4

Chicory/Belgian endive is such an underrated vegetable, unlike in France and Italy where they use it a lot, and not just in the salad bowl. It is so different when cooked, becoming silky smooth and slightly bitter, which is why it works so well against a sweet, smoky ham like Black Forest ham. The chilli and lemon in the dressing wake up all the flavours. If you make this once you'll be addicted.

Preheat the oven to low.

To make the dressing, put the garlic, chilli and vinegar in a bowl and whisk in the olive oil and lemon zest and juice.

Heat the butter in a large frying pan over low heat and add the chicory/endive, cut side down. Season with salt and pepper, cover with a lid and let cook gently for 5–6 minutes. Remove the lid, turn up the heat and continue to cook for 5 minutes, until the chicory/endive is golden. Turn the chicory/endive halves over and cook for 3–4 minutes so the other side gets a chance to caramelize. Keep warm in the oven.

Fill a large, deep frying pan with water and bring to a simmer. Crack the eggs around the edge so they don't touch and poach for exactly 3 minutes.

Place a mound of rocket/arugula on each plate, top with 2 chicory/endive halves and drape the Black Forest ham on top. Scoop out each poached egg and place on top of the ham. Scatter some Parmesan shavings around the plate and finish with a drizzle of dressing.

French toast with provolone & half-dried tomatoes

4 eggs

175 ml/⅔ cup whole milk

4 thick slices of challah

1 tablespoon pesto

100 g/3½ oz. Provolone or
mozzarella, thinly sliced

6 half-dried tomatoes,
chopped

a handful of fresh basil
leaves

2 tablespoons olive oil

sea salt and freshly ground
black pepper

SERVES 4

French toast works really well as a savoury dish, too. This one is not dissimilar to the Italian *mozzarella in carrozza*, where a mozzarella sandwich dipped in egg is fried. You can vary the filling, adding ham or salami if you like. The important thing is that you soak the bread so it absorbs all the egg and finish it off in the oven after frying as it won't cook all the way through like a thin French toast.

Preheat the oven to 180°C (350°F) Gas 4.

Put the eggs and milk in a bowl and whisk together with a little salt and pepper. Using a paring knife, make a pocket in each slice of challah by cutting horizontally into the middle of one of the long sides. Spread a quarter of the pesto on the inside of each pocket, then fill with the provolone, tomatoes and basil. Place in a shallow dish, pour in the egg mixture and set aside for 10 minutes.

Heat the oil in a frying pan over high heat and fry the bread for 1–2 minutes on each side, until golden. Transfer to a baking sheet and bake in the preheated oven for 10 minutes, until puffed up.

Caramelized chicory/belgian endive with black forest ham & poached eggs (right)

Omelette with chives & gruyère

3 eggs

2 tablespoons snipped
   fresh chives

1 tablespoon butter

2 tablespoons Gruyère,
   grated

1 tablespoon double/heavy
   cream

sea salt and freshly ground
   black pepper

20-cm/8-in. frying pan

SERVES 1

A perfectly crumpled, soft omelette oozing with cheese is bliss. Too many omelettes are cooked badly, but once you master the technique, there's no end of combinations you can make. I love this indulgent filling, which complements, as opposed to overpowering the egg element of the omelette.

Gently beat the eggs in a bowl and season with salt and pepper. Stir in half the chives.

Heat the frying pan over high heat until really hot. Add the butter, wait for it to sizzle, then just as it wants to brown pour in the eggs. Let them become nicely golden on the outside – no more than 45 seconds – drawing the cooked edges into the centre. Tilt the pan so the uncooked egg runs into the edges. When the omelette is evenly set, except for a little unset egg, it is done.

Remove the pan from the heat and add the Gruyère and cream in the middle. Fold 2 edges of the omelette over, then tilt the pan so you can slide it out and upturn it onto a plate, seam side down. Grind some pepper over the top and finish with the remaining chives.

Smoked haddock, radish & avocado omelette wraps

6 eggs

about 2 tablespoons butter

200 g/6½ oz. hot smoked
   haddock, flaked

2 handfuls of watercress

1 ripe avocado, peeled,
   pitted and chopped

6 radishes, thinly sliced

2 tablespoons extra virgin
   olive oil

2 tablespoons lemon juice

sea salt and freshly ground
   black pepper

15–18-cm/6–7-in. frying pan

SERVES 4

These wraps are a cross between a pancake and an omelette. You can use any smoked fish for this, but I like hot smoked fish as this dispenses with cooking it first. Salmon, mackerel and eel would all work just as well as the haddock I've used here. Make sure the avocado is soft and ripe and season it really well.

Preheat the oven to low.

Gently beat the eggs in a bowl and season with salt and pepper. Put an ovenproof plate in the oven to heat up.

Heat about 1 teaspoon of the butter in the frying pan over high heat and swirl it around the pan. Pour in about 3 tablespoons of the beaten eggs – just enough to coat the base of the pan. Wait for 30 seconds, then flip over. Repeat with the remaining mixture, using the same amount of butter each time, until you have about 8 omelettes, keeping them warm on the plate in the oven.

Meanwhile, place the smoked haddock, watercress, avocado and radishes in a large mixing bowl. Stir in the oil and lemon juice and season with pepper.

Lay 2 omelettes out on a board and spoon some of the haddock filling down the middle of each one, then roll up and transfer to a plate. Repeat with the remaining wraps and 3 more plates.

Smoked haddock, radish & avocado omelette wraps (left)

Tortilla with potatoes, chillies & peppers

6 tablespoons olive oil

600 g/1¼ lbs. (about 4) potatoes, peeled and thinly sliced

2 red chillies, thinly sliced

1 onion, thinly sliced

½ teaspoon sea salt

8 eggs

125 g/4 oz. marinated roasted pimento peppers

deep 20-cm/8-in. nonstick frying pan

SERVES 6

The secret of a good tortilla is to soften the potatoes in lots of olive oil and then add them to the eggs and back into the pan, not the other way around. If you pour the eggs directly over the potatoes in the pan, they will not coat the potatoes evenly and you will get air bubbles. Don't rush the cooking either – the egg proteins will get agitated, resulting in a tough texture rather than a creamy finish.

Heat 4 tablespoons of the oil in the frying pan, then add the potatoes, chillies, onion and salt. Reduce the heat to low and cover with a lid. Cook for 15 minutes, stirring occasionally so the onions don't catch on the base of the pan.

Preheat the grill/broiler.

Beat the eggs in a large mixing bowl. Transfer the cooked ingredients from the frying pan to the beaten eggs and stir.

Drain and chop the roasted peppers, then add to the egg mixture.

Turn the heat up to medium under the frying pan and add the remaining oil. Pour the egg mixture into the pan. Cook for 4–5 minutes until the base is golden – loosen the sides and lift up to check.

Grill/broil for 3–4 minutes, until it is cooked all the way through. Cut into wedges and serve.

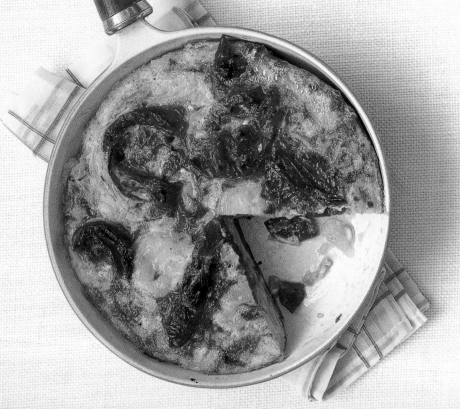

Wild mushroom mini-frittatas with garlic sourdough croutons

50 g/½ cup grated
   Parmesan, plus extra
   for dusting
25 g/1 oz. dried porcini
   mushrooms
25 g/2 tablespoons butter
3 shallots, finely chopped
2 garlic cloves, crushed
300 g/10 oz. wild
   mushrooms, such as
   chantereiles and
   trompettes
leaves from 2 sprigs of
   fresh thyme
8 eggs
sea salt and freshly ground
   black pepper
watercress, to serve

CROUTONS
2 slices of sourdough, torn
   into 2-cm/1-in. chunks,
   crust and all
4 tablespoons olive oil
1 garlic clove, crushed
*9-hole muffin pan with
   large holes*

MAKES 9

Frittatas look so cute when they are baked in a muffin pan. Make this at the end of the summer when wild mushrooms are cheap and plentiful. The sourdough croutons add a good contrast in texture.

Preheat the oven to 190°C (375°F) Gas 5. Grease the muffin pan and dust with Parmesan. Put the porcini in a little bowl with 2 tablespoons boiling water and let soak for 15 minutes.

To make the croutons, put the sourdough in a roasting pan, toss with the oil, garlic and seasoning and roast in the preheated oven for 20 minutes.

Melt the butter in a frying pan, then add the shallots and sauté over low heat for 5–6 minutes, until softened. Add the garlic and wild mushrooms, turn up the heat and cook for 3–4 minutes, until they become tender and any moisture has evaporated. Season well and add the thyme. Gently beat the eggs in a mixing bowl. Drain the soaked porcini and add to the eggs with the cooked ingredients from the pan, the Parmesan and some seasoning and beat. Divide between the muffin pan holes, dust with more Parmesan and cook in the preheated oven for 18–20 minutes, until just set.

Let stand for 5 minutes, then serve with watercress and the croutons.

pastries & bakes

Walnut bread with goat cheese, honey & wet walnuts Easy sourdough bread **Jalapeño & cheddar cornbread** Lemon & raisin soda bread Chocolate chip banana bread **Marmalade & almond bread** Crumpets Poppyseed bagels **Sticky cinnamon & cardamom palmiers** Jam & frangipane brioches Dairy-free banana, date & bran muffins **Exploding berry crumble muffins** Sugary jam doughnut muffins Chocolate chip & peanut butter muffins **Brioche french toast with pineapple & syrup** Apple streusel coffee cake Pecan & maple syrup sticky buns **Churros with cinnamon sugar** Apple turnovers

Walnut bread with goat cheese, honey & wet walnuts

75 g/⅓ cup (clear) honey, plus extra to serve

7 g/1 envelope dried active yeast

500 ml/2 cups warm water

100 g/6½ tablespoons butter, melted

4 tablespoons walnut oil

200 g/1¼ cups shelled dried walnuts, chopped

1 tablespoon sea salt

750 g wholemeal bread flour/4 cups whole-wheat flour and 1½ cups bread flour, plus extra for dusting

400 g/13 oz. fresh goat cheese, to serve

a handful of wet (fresh) walnuts, or dried, to serve

2 baking sheets, dusted with flour

MAKES 2 X 450-G/1-LB. LOAVES

In autumn when wet (fresh) walnuts abound, this is the most delicious way to serve them. The bread is quite sweet so it makes a lovely breakfast treat with chalky fresh goat cheese and a bowl of wet walnuts. I like to serve these in their shells, which forces people to interact with the food and heightens the enjoyment.

Put the honey, yeast and water in a large bowl. Set aside in a draught-free place for 15 minutes until foamy on the surface. Pour in the butter, oil, walnuts and salt.

Place the flour in a food mixer with a dough hook attachment. Alternatively, do this by hand. Set the mixer to the lowest speed and stir in the foamy mixture. The dough should be soft and slightly sticky. Turn the mixer up (or use elbow grease!) and knead the dough for 10–15 minutes. Place in a clean, lightly oiled bowl, cover with plastic wrap and leave in a warm place for 1 hour, or until it has doubled in size.

Gently push the air out of the dough and take it out of the bowl, keeping the top as untouched as possible as this will be the structure of your crust. Slice the dough in half, shape into ovals and smooth the edges by drawing the rough edges underneath and pinching them together on the underside. The top should be smooth and slightly stretched. Transfer to the prepared baking sheets, cover with a dish cloth and rest for 20–30 minutes, until doubled in size. Preheat the oven to 230°C (450°F) Gas 8.

Dust the bread generously with flour and score the top with diagonal lines. Sprinkle the sides of the oven with a little water. Bake the bread in the preheated oven for 5 minutes, then reduce the heat to 200°C (400°F) Gas 6 and bake for a further 25–30 minutes, until golden brown and hollow-sounding when tapped underneath. Let cool on a wire rack.

Easy sourdough bread

400 g/3¼ cups rye flour

2 teaspoons sea salt

200 ml/¾ cup warm water

20 g/¾ oz. fresh yeast or
  1 tablespoon dried
  active yeast

250 g/2 cups strong
  wholemeal bread flour/
  whole-wheat flour

250 g/2 cups strong white
  /bread flour, plus extra
  for dusting

*2 baking sheets, dusted
  with flour*

**MAKES 2 X 450-G/1-LB.
LOAVES**

Real sourdough takes several days of commitment; as in the method below, you make a starter from flour and water and leave it until it begins to ferment and give off a tangy, alcoholic aroma. However, from here, you have to feed the starter to encourage the yeast to multiply. I have skipped this stage and just added the starter to the bread dough so that you get the tangy flavour without the wait.

To make the starter, put 150 g/1¼ cups of the rye flour, the salt and water in a large bowl. Cover with clingfilm/plastic wrap and leave at room temperature for 36 hours, by which time it should smell slightly tangy.

When you are ready to start making the dough, blend the yeast with 200 ml/¾ cup hand-hot water (crumble it in if it is fresh yeast or sprinkle if it is dried). Transfer the remaining rye flour, and the wholemeal/whole-wheat and white/bread flours to a food mixer with a dough hook attachment. Alternatively, do this by hand. Set the mixer to the lowest speed and stir in the yeast mixture, followed by the sourdough starter, adding a little more warm water if it is still dry to achieve a soft, slightly sticky dough.

Turn the mixer up (or use some elbow grease!) and knead the dough for 10–15 minutes. Place in a clean, lightly oiled bowl, cover with clingfilm/plastic wrap and leave in a warm place for 1–2 hours, until almost doubled in size.

Gently push the air out of the dough and take it out of the bowl, keeping the top as untouched as possible as this will be the structure of your crust. Slice the dough in half and smooth the edges by drawing the rough edges underneath and pinching them together on the underside. The top should be smooth and slightly stretched, and the loaf round. Transfer to the prepared baking sheets, cover with a dish cloth and let rest for 1 hour, until doubled in size.

Meanwhile, preheat the oven to 230°C (450°F) Gas 8.

Dust the bread generously with flour and score the top with a criss-cross pattern. Sprinkle the sides of the oven with a little water. Bake the bread in the preheated oven for 5 minutes, then reduce the heat to 200°C (400°F) Gas 6 and bake for a further 25–30 minutes, until golden brown and hollow-sounding when tapped underneath. Let cool on a wire rack.

Jalapeño & cheddar cornbread

150 g/1¼ cups plain/all-purpose flour

2 teaspoons bicarbonate of/baking soda

1 teaspoon sea salt

150 g/1 cup medium cornmeal or polenta

2 tablespoons (caster) sugar

150 g/1¼ cups grated sharp cheddar

2 jalapeño peppers

275 ml/1¼ cups buttermilk

50 g/3 tablespoons butter, melted

1 egg, beaten

22-cm/9-in. round cake pan, greased

SERVES 6–8

Cornbread is not really a bread at all but a crumbly, buttery cake which can be served with fried chicken, or buttered and eaten for breakfast with a strong black coffee. It makes a nice change next to a plate of baked beans too, especially if they're homemade, such as the ones on page 128.

Preheat the oven to 190°C (375°F) Gas 5.

Sift the flour and bicarbonate of/baking soda into a mixing bowl and stir in the salt, cornmeal, sugar, and cheddar. Chop the jalapeño peppers and add those to the bowl too.

In another bowl, beat together the buttermilk, butter and egg. Pour into the dry ingredients and briefly fold in until no floury pockets remain. Scrape into the prepared cake pan and bake in the preheated oven for 20–25 minutes, until a skewer inserted into the centre comes out clean. Let cool in the pan for 5 minutes, then turn out onto a wire rack to cool completely.

Lemon & raisin soda bread

150 g/1 cup raisins

400 g wholemeal flour/2 cups whole-wheat and 1 cup all-purpose flour, plus extra for dusting

2 teaspoons bicarbonate of/baking soda

2 tablespoons sugar

1 teaspoon sea salt

250 ml/1 cup buttermilk

finely grated zest of 1 unwaxed lemon

baking sheet, lightly floured

22-cm/9-in. round cake pan

SERVES 6–8

This soda bread is studded with raisins and streaked with lemon zest, making it even more delicious than plain soda bread. It is one of the easiest breads to make because it requires no yeast, using baking soda as a raising agent. I like to toast it and slather it with butter and a preserve from the last chapter of the book.

Preheat the oven to 220°C (425°F) Gas 7.

Soak the raisins in 200 ml/¾ cup water for 15 minutes.

Put the flour, bicarbonate of/baking soda, sugar and salt in a large mixing bowl. Make a well in the middle and pour in the buttermilk, zest, raisins and their water, gradually drawing in the floury mixture with a wooden spoon until you have a soft, slightly loose but not sticky dough.

Bring the dough together with your hands and shape into a round roughly 22 cm/9 inches across and 5 cm/2 inches deep. Don't knead or overwork the dough.

Place on the prepared baking sheet and score a large cross across the surface of the bread with a sharp knife. Dust with flour. Place the cake pan, upturned, on top of the bread to prevent it from browning too much. Bake in the preheated oven for 15 minutes. Reduce the heat to 200°C (400°F) Gas 6, remove the cake pan from on top of the bread and bake for a further 10–15 minutes, until it is hollow-sounding when tapped underneath. Let cool on a wire rack.

Jalapeño & cheddar cornbread (right)

Chocolate chip banana bread

225 g/1¾ cups plain/
  all-purpose flour
1 teaspoon baking powder
½ teaspoon salt
175 g/¾ cup packed light
  brown sugar
4 over-ripe bananas, mashed
85 g/5½ tablespoons
  butter, melted
2 large eggs, lightly beaten
100 g/⅔ cup chopped dark
  chocolate
900-g/2-lb. loaf pan, greased
  and baselined with baking
  parchment

SERVES 8–10

This is a cake that can't go wrong, unless you are not patient enough to wait for the bananas to ripen. This is a real no-no; they have to be black to get that deep flavour. In fact, in our house, we make this loaf to suit the look of our bananas, not the other way round. Saying that, we seem to let them go black a lot more than we need to, in anticipation of this cake. The chocolate chips are just gilding the lily but when they come out molten and oozy it makes the bread irresistible.

Preheat the oven to 180°C (350°F) Gas 4.

Put the flour, baking powder and salt in a mixing bowl. In another bowl, mix the sugar and bananas until there are no large lumps. Beat in the butter and eggs.

Tip the wet ingredients into the dry ingredients and mix, being careful not to overmix otherwise the bread will be tough. Stir in the chocolate. Spoon the thick batter into the prepared loaf pan and bake in the middle of the preheated oven for 40–45 minutes, until a skewer inserted into the middle comes out clean.

Let the bread cool in the pan for 10 minutes, then turn out onto a wire rack to cool completely. When cold, serve in slices with butter or a decadent dollop of ricotta.

Marmalade & almond bread

This is a moist cake streaked with zesty marmalade and kept moist by the addition of ground almonds. Be careful not to cook this in a very hot oven as the sugar content is high and the outside likes to brown. Serve it in chunky slices with Earl Grey tea.

225 g/2 sticks butter, soft

150 g/³⁄₄ cup (golden caster) sugar

juice of ¹⁄₂ orange

finely grated zest of 1 orange

130 g/¹⁄₂ cup orange marmalade

4 large eggs

150 g/1 cup plus 2 tablespoons self-raising flour

75 g/¹⁄₂ cup ground almonds

900-g/2-lb. loaf pan, greased and baselined with baking parchment

SERVES 8–10

Preheat the oven to 170°C (325°F) Gas 3.

Put the butter and sugar in a large mixing bowl and beat with an electric handheld whisk until the mixture is pale and light. Gradually add the orange juice, zest and the marmalade and swirl through with the whisk.

Lightly beat the eggs with a fork in a small bowl. Keep the electric whisk running in the creamed butter bowl and trickle the eggs in, 1 tablespoon at a time, beating thoroughly after each addition to stop them curdling. Finally, fold in the flour and ground almonds. Spoon the mixture into the prepared loaf pan and bake on a low shelf in the preheated oven for about 45 minutes, until lightly golden on top. A skewer inserted in the middle should come out clean.

Let the bread cool in the pan for 15 minutes, then transfer to a wire rack to cool completely. It is easier to slice when it's cold – if you can resist its alluring aroma while it cools.

Crumpets

500 ml/2 cups whole milk

1 teaspoon sugar

20 g/³⁄₄ oz. fresh yeast or 1 tablespoon dried active yeast

200 g/1½ cups strong white/bread flour

200 g/1½ cups plain/all-purpose flour

1 teaspoon salt

2 tablespoons sunflower oil

250 ml/1 cup warm water

½ teaspoon bicarbonate of/baking soda

4 x 8-cm/3-in. metal rings, greased

MAKES 12

Making crumpets is like reverting back to the childhood days of chemistry sets – you may not understand the chemical reaction happening, but it's great to see the crumpets bubble, ready to receive melted butter in their pockets.

Pour the milk and sugar into a saucepan and heat until warm. Remove from the heat, scatter over the yeast and set aside for 10 minutes until foamy on the surface.

Sift the flours and salt into a mixing bowl and add the oil and wet, foamy mixture. Beat with an electric handheld whisk for 3 minutes, or until smooth. Cover with clingfilm/plastic wrap and leave for 1½–2 hours, until it has doubled in size and is covered in tiny bubbles.

Mix the water and bicarbonate of/baking soda until dissolved. Using the electric whisk, beat this into the risen dough until smooth. Cover again and let rise for a further 20 minutes.

Put the metal rings on a hot non-stick frying pan. Spoon 2 tablespoons of the batter into each ring so they are half full. Cook over very low heat for 5–7 minutes until the surface is pockmarked and dry around the edges. Slide the rings off, flip the crumpets over and cook for 1 minute, until pale gold. Wrap in a clean dish cloth while you cook the rest. Serve with butter and runny raspberry jam.

Poppyseed bagels

7 g/1 envelope dried active yeast

4 tablespoons clear honey

300 ml/1¼ cups warm water

450 g/3½ cups strong white/bread flour

1 teaspoon salt

2 teaspoons bicarbonate of/baking soda

2 tablespoons poppyseeds

baking sheet, lined with baking parchment

MAKES 10

Moist chewy bagels are made from a fairly standard white dough, but they are poached before being baked. I like to smother them in cream cheese and excessive amounts of raspberry jam for that sweet and savoury contrast.

Put the yeast in a small bowl with the honey and 100 ml/½ cup of the water. Set aside for 10 minutes until frothy.

Put the flour and salt in a bowl and make a well in the middle. Pour in the frothy mixture and draw the flour into the liquid with a wooden spoon. Add more warm water and mix until you get a soft dough. It should not be very sticky. Turn out onto a lightly floured surface and knead for 10 minutes. Return to the bowl, cover and leave for 20 minutes.

Divide the dough into 10 equal pieces. Shape each piece into a flattish ball, then take a wooden spoon and use the handle to make a hole in the middle of each ball. Twirl the bagel around the spoon to make a hole 3 cm/1½ inches wide. Lay the bagels on the baking sheet and cover. Set aside for 30–45 minutes.

Preheat the oven to 230°C (450°F) Gas 8.

Bring a large pan of salted water to the boil and add the bicarbonate of/baking soda. Poach 3 bagels at a time for 30 seconds on each side. Fish out, drain off any excess water and scatter with poppyseeds. Place on the baking sheet. Bake for 10 minutes until lightly golden and cooked through.

Crumpets (right)

Sticky cinnamon & cardamom palmiers

6 cardamom pods

6 tablespoons demerara
    sugar

1 teaspoon ground
    cinnamon

4 tablespoons poppyseeds

375 g/12 oz. puff pastry
    dough, thawed if frozen

1 egg, beaten

nonstick baking sheet

MAKES 16

These little sugary pastries are ideal as a mid-morning snack with a strong black coffee. You can vary the spices or omit the cardamom and leave them plain.

Put the cardamom pods in a freezer bag and crush them to separate the pale green husks from the black seeds inside. Discard the husks and crush the seeds with the sugar using a pestle and mortar, just until they break up a little. Transfer to a small bowl with the ground cinnamon and poppyseeds.

Roll out the pastry dough on a lightly floured work surface into a rectangle approximately 60 x 30 cm/24 x 12 inches. Brush all over with the beaten egg and scatter half the dry ingredients over the top. Fold the two shorter edges over to meet in the middle. Brush with more egg

wash and scatter with the remaining dry ingredients. Bring the new outside ends over again to join in the middle. Fold the pastry in half as if you were closing a book. Lift onto the nonstick baking sheet, then gently press down so you have a rectangular log with pleated folds. Refrigerate for 30 minutes. Preheat the oven to 200°C (400°F) Gas 6.

Remove from the fridge and cut into 1.5-cm/½-inch slices. Return each slice, flat side down, to the baking sheet with some room to expand. Bake in the preheated oven for 18–20 minutes, until golden. Let cool on a wire rack.

Jam & frangipane brioches

These are a cross between an English Bakewell tart and an old French recipe for using up stale brioche, called Bostock. They are surprisingly easy to whip up and are wonderful for a decadent breakfast. They will keep for a couple of days and can be polished off at teatime or warmed and eaten with cream for dessert.

75 g/5 tablespoons
   unsalted butter, soft
75 g/⅓ cup (caster) sugar
1 egg yolk
75 g/½ cup ground
   almonds
75 g/⅓ cup raspberry,
   rhubarb or apricot jam
6 stale brioche fingers
   or 4 stale brioche buns,
   halved
3 tablespoons flaked/
   slivered almonds
baking sheet, lined with
   baking parchment

MAKES 8–12

Preheat the oven to 190°C (375°F) Gas 5.

To make what is effectively frangipane, put the butter and sugar in a bowl and beat with an electric handheld whisk until light and fluffy. Beat in the egg yolk in 2 stages (so that it doesn't curdle), then fold in the ground almonds.

Spread the jam over the cut sides of the brioche, then spread a blob of frangipane on top. Scatter with the flaked/slivered almonds. Transfer to the prepared baking sheet and bake in the preheated oven for 10–12 minutes, until the topping is puffed up and tinged with brown.

Dairy-free banana, date & bran muffins

150 g/1 cup plus 2 tablespoons wholemeal/whole-wheat flour

100 g/²⁄₃ cup plus 2 tablespoons wheat bran

a pinch of salt

2 teaspoons ground cinnamon

2 teaspoons baking powder

2 eggs

75 g/¹⁄₃ cup clear honey

200 ml/¾ cup soya milk

75 ml/¹⁄₃ cup vegetable oil

150 g/1 cup pitted dates, chopped

3 bananas, sliced

12-hole muffin pan

MAKES 10–12

These muffins are full of fibre and super filling. As with all muffins, they need to be stirred with a hand that is not too worried about getting every last lump out, as this rocky batter gives them their characteristically clumpy, rough texture.

Preheat the oven to 180°C (350°F) Gas 4. Line the muffin pan with paper cases.

Sift the flour, 80 g/²⁄₃ cup of the wheat bran, the salt, cinnamon and baking powder into a large mixing bowl.

Beat the eggs with the honey, soya milk and oil. Pour the wet ingredients into the dry ingredients and scatter the dates and bananas on top. Using a large spoon, fold until the mixture is moistened. It needs to be lumpy and shouldn't be overworked otherwise the baked muffins will be tough. Spoon into the paper cases until they are two-thirds full and scatter over the reserved bran. Bake in the preheated oven for 18–22 minutes.

Let cool in the pan for 5 minutes before transferring to a wire rack.

Exploding berry crumble muffins

375 g/2¾ cups plain/all-purpose flour

3 teaspoons baking powder

1 teaspoon bicarbonate of/baking soda

150 g/¾ cup (caster) sugar

½ teaspoon salt

2 eggs, beaten

115 g/1 stick unsalted butter, melted

200 g/¾ cup sour cream

60 ml/¼ cup whole milk

180 g/1¼ cups raspberries

TOPPING

100 g/¾ cup plain/all-purpose flour

75 g/5 tablespoons butter, chilled and cubed

2 tablespoons sugar

3 tablespoons flaked/slivered almonds

12-hole muffin pan

MAKES 12

These look like the muffins which are sold in cafés and which seem to have exploded out of their pans with their generous proportions. There is no secret trick to this – just fill the paper cases up to the top.

Preheat the oven to 170°C (325°F) Gas 3. Line the muffin pan with paper cases and grease the surface of the pan where the muffins will rise and stick.

To make the topping, put the flour and butter in a food processor and pulse briefly, just until the butter is blended. Tip out into a bowl and add the sugar and almonds, pressing the mixture together with your hands.

To make the muffins, sift the flour, baking powder, bicarbonate of/baking soda, sugar and salt into a large mixing bowl. Put the eggs in a bowl, add the melted butter, sour cream and milk and whisk to combine. Pour the wet ingredients into the dry ingredients and scatter the raspberries on top. Using a large spoon, fold until the mixture is moistened. It needs to be lumpy and shouldn't be overworked. Spoon into the paper cases right to the top. For regular-sized (not exploding!) muffins you can spoon the cases two-thirds full – you will be able to make more of these with this amount of mixture. Finish by scattering over the topping.

Bake in the preheated oven for 25–28 minutes for large muffins, or 18–22 minutes for the smaller ones.

Let cool for 5 minutes in the pan before transferring to a wire rack.

Exploding berry crumble muffins (right)

75 ml/¹⁄₃ cup sunflower oil

150 g/²⁄₃ cup plain yogurt

¹⁄₂ teaspoon vanilla extract

2 large eggs, beaten

275 g/2 cups plus 2
    tablespoons self-raising
    flour

¹⁄₂ teaspoon bicarbonate
    of/baking soda

a pinch of salt

100 g/¹⁄₂ cup (caster) sugar

75 g/¹⁄₃ cup blueberry jam

TOPPING

25 g/2 tablespoons
    unsalted butter, melted

50 g/¹⁄₄ cup (caster) sugar

6-hole muffin pan,
    lined with paper cases

MAKES 6

Sugary jam doughnut muffins

This is a recipe for anyone who likes a warm sugary doughnut but dislikes the deep frying involved in making them. Of course the result is more cakey than bready but they are every bit as delicious, as they ooze jam and cover your lips with sugar crystals.

Preheat the oven to 190°C (375°F) Gas 5.

Put the oil, yogurt, vanilla extract and eggs in a bowl and beat together.

In another, large bowl, mix together the flour, bicarbonate of/baking soda, salt and sugar. Pour the wet ingredients into the dry ingredients and mix together until just combined. It needs to be quite lumpy but you need to hassle any floury pockets until there are no more.

Drop 1 big tablespoon of the batter in each paper case. Make a dip in the mixture and spoon in a big teaspoon of the jam. Divide the remaining batter between the paper cases to cover the jam. Bake in the preheated oven for 18–20 minutes, until well risen. Set aside, still in the pan, to cool for 5 minutes before you apply the topping.

When the muffins have cooled for 5 minutes, brush their tops with the melted butter for the topping and roll in the sugar. Transfer to a wire rack to cool to room temperature.

250 g/2 cups plain/all-
    purpose flour

2 teaspoons baking powder

¹⁄₂ teaspoon bicarbonate
    of/baking soda

75 g/¹⁄₃ cup (caster) sugar

250 g/1 cup crunchy
    peanut butter

1 large egg, beaten

50 g/3¹⁄₂ tablespoons
    butter, melted

100 g/¹⁄₂ cup plain yogurt

100 ml/¹⁄₃ cup whole milk

100 g/²⁄₃ cup milk
    chocolate chips

12-hole muffin pan,
    lined with paper cases

MAKES 12

Chocolate chip & peanut butter muffins

You can't really go wrong with salty peanuts and sweet chocolate. If you love Reese's Pieces, then this is the muffin you've been waiting for. For these indulgent muffins, I prefer the creamy sweetness of milk chocolate, rather than the more refined dark chocolate I usually use for baking.

Preheat the oven to 180°C (350°F) Gas 4.

Sift the flour, baking powder and bicarbonate of/baking soda into a large mixing bowl, then add the sugar and crunchy peanut butter.

Put the egg, melted butter, yogurt and milk in a bowl and beat together. Stir in the chocolate chips. Pour the wet ingredients into the dry ingredients.

Using a large spoon, fold until the mixture is moistened. It needs to be lumpy and shouldn't be overworked otherwise the baked muffins will be tough. Spoon into the paper cases until they are two-thirds full. Bake in the preheated oven for 20–22 minutes, until golden and well risen.

Let cool in the pan for 5 minutes before transferring to a wire rack.

Sugary jam doughnut muffins (left)

Brioche french toast with pineapple & syrup

1 vanilla pod/bean, split
    lengthways

100 g/½ cup packed light
    brown sugar

2 cinnamon sticks

6 eggs, beaten

100 ml/6 tablespoons
    whole milk

8 thick slices of brioche

25 g/2 tablespoons butter

3 tablespoons sunflower
    oil

1 pineapple, peeled, cored
    and sliced into rounds

SERVES 4

Light, buttery brioche makes wonderful French toast. As it is so rich, a slightly tart fruit is needed – I like to griddle slices of pineapple and drench them in syrup.

Scrape the seeds out of the vanilla pod/bean. Put half the seeds, the pod/bean, the sugar, 200 ml/¾ cup water and the cinnamon in a saucepan over low heat and heat gently until the sugar has dissolved. Turn up the heat and simmer for 10 minutes, until syrupy. Put the eggs, milk and remaining vanilla seeds in a wide bowl and whisk together lightly. Dip the brioche in the egg mixture, transfer to a plate and let soak up all the mixture.

Heat half the butter and oil in your largest frying pan over medium heat. Add as many slices of soaked bread as you can and cook for 2–3 minutes on each side. Repeat until all the bread is fried.

Heat a ridged stovetop grill pan over high heat and brush the pineapple with a little of the syrup. Grill for 2 minutes on each side. Serve 2 slices of French toast with a couple of slices of pineapple and a drizzle of the syrup.

Apple streusel coffee cake

150 g/10 tablespoons
    butter, soft

150 g/¾ cup (caster) sugar

2 large eggs, beaten

2 teaspoons vanilla extract

100 g/¾ cup plain/all-
    purpose flour, sifted

½ teaspoon baking powder

½ teaspoon bicarbonate
    of/baking soda

100 g/⅔ cup ground almonds

100 g/½ cup sour cream

3 dessert apples, peeled,
    cored and thinly sliced

TOPPING

75 g/⅔ cup plain/all-
    purpose flour

75 g/⅓ cup light brown sugar

½ teaspoon ground cinnamon

3 tablespoons butter, soft

100 g/⅔ cup chopped pecans

20-cm/8-in. round cake pan

SERVES 8

This is a coffee cake in the sense that it is good with a mid-morning coffee. The cake mixture is really vanillary and stays a little bit moist around the apples as they let off their steam. I adore the contrast of this against the nutty, crunchy topping. A strong coffee and a gossip are all you need to accessorize this delight.

Preheat the oven to 180°C (350°F) Gas 4. Line the cake pan with baking parchment.

Cream the butter and sugar with an electric handheld whisk until fluffy. Gradually beat in the eggs and vanilla extract, then fold in the flour, baking powder, bicarbonate of/baking soda and almonds. Beat in the sour cream until you have a dropping consistency. Spoon half the batter into the prepared pan. Arrange the apples snugly on top, in a single layer, and spoon over the remaining batter.

To make the topping, put the flour, sugar and cinnamon in a bowl and rub in the butter with your fingertips until the mixture is crumbly. Add 1 tablespoon water and the pecans and break into lumps with a blunt knife. Scatter this over the cake and bake in the preheated oven for 50–60 minutes. A skewer inserted in the middle of the cake should come out clean. If it doesn't, bake for a few minutes more before checking again (noting that the apples will make it seem quite wet).

Let the cake to cool in the pan for 10 minutes, then transfer to a wire rack to cool completely. Alternatively, enjoy it with cream while it is still warm.

Apple streusel coffee cake (right)

Pecan & maple syrup sticky buns

250 ml/1 cup whole milk,
plus extra for glazing

85 g/6 tablespoons
unsalted butter

500 g/3¾ cups strong
white/bread flour

50 g/¼ cup packed light
brown sugar

7 g/1 envelope easy-blend/
rapid-rise dried yeast

½ teaspoon salt

1 egg, beaten

FILLING

75 g/5 tablespoons
unsalted butter, softened

75 ml/⅓ cup pure maple
syrup

75 g/⅓ cup packed light
brown sugar

1 tablespoon ground
cinnamon

100 g/⅔ cup chopped
pecans

MAKES ABOUT 16

It's quite fun to make your own sticky buns, but you need to start the day before unless you are a hopeless insomniac. This dough is enriched with butter and egg and is ready to bake when it is like a soft, puffy marshmallow. Try putting different nuts, chocolate chips and/or dried fruit in the middle for a change. They are best served warm on the day they are made, so if you are eating them after that, warm them a little in the oven first to soften up.

Put the milk and butter in a saucepan and heat gently until the butter has melted. Remove from the heat and let cool until blood temperature. Put the flour, sugar, yeast and salt in a large bowl.

Pour the egg into the cooled milk and beat. Make a well in the middle of the dry ingredients and pour in the milk mixture. Gradually draw in the floury mixture with a wooden spoon until it is all combined. Bring the dough together with your hands, then tip out onto a lightly floured work surface and knead for 10 minutes, until smooth and the dough springs back when poked. Place in a lightly oiled bowl and cover with clingfilm/plastic wrap. Let rise for 1–2 hours.

Meanwhile, to make the filling, mix the butter, maple syrup, sugar, cinnamon and pecans in a small bowl and set aside.

Push the air out of the dough and lay it on the work surface. Using the heel of your hand, flatten and shape it into a rectangle about 30 × 40 cm/12 × 16 inches. Spread the filling over the surface of the dough. With one of the long sides facing you, roll up the dough like a Swiss jelly roll and refrigerate for 1 hour.

Cut the roll into 2-cm/¾-inch slices. Arrange these, flat side down, on a baking sheet spaced about 2 cm/1 inch apart so that they have room to expand. Cover loosely with clingfilm/plastic wrap and let rise for 30 minutes, until puffy. Preheat the oven to 200°C (400°F) Gas 6.

Brush the buns with milk and slide into the oven. Immediately reduce the heat to 180°C (350°F) Gas 4 and bake for 12–15 minutes, until cooked through and golden.

Churros with cinnamon sugar

50 g/3 tablespoons butter
2 tablespoons (caster)
    sugar
125 g/1 cup plain/all-
    purpose flour
a pinch of salt
2 large eggs, beaten
about 750 ml/3 cups
    vegetable oil, for deep
    frying

CINNAMON SUGAR

6 tablespoons (caster)
    sugar
1 teaspoon ground
    cinnamon
piping bag, fitted with a
    1.5-cm/½-in. star-shaped
    nozzle/tip
MAKES 12

These Spanish morsels of deliciousness are a bit like doughnuts. Making them is a little like making French choux pastry, except that the batter is then squeezed out of a piping bag into boiling hot oil. I know this all sounds like a labour of love but there is nothing better on a rainy day than to enjoy them with a cup of hot chocolate. When they cool down, they lose a lot of their magic.

Put the butter, sugar and 150 ml/⅔ cup water in a small saucepan and bring to the boil. Tip the flour and salt into the boiling water, remove from the heat and beat vigorously with a wooden spoon for 20 seconds, until the mixture comes away from the sides of the pan and forms a clump. Let cool for 10 minutes or until it is lukewarm.

Beat in the eggs, a spoonful at a time. Cover, refrigerate and let cool completely.

Fill a large saucepan one-third full with vegetable oil. Heat to 190°C/375°F (or until a dot of the churros batter bubbles up and floats straightaway). Spoon the batter into the prepared piping bag. Squeeze 3 x 9-cm/3½-inch lengths of batter into the hot oil. (Use your finger to release the batter from the nozzle of the piping bag.) Fry for 2 minutes on each side until golden. Drain on kitchen paper/paper towels and fry the remaining batter in the same way.

To make the cinnamon sugar, mix the sugar and cinnamon in a large, wide dish. Roll the churros in the mixture while they are hot and oily, until evenly coated. Serve with hot chocolate or coffee.

Apple turnovers

25 g/2 tablespoons unsalted butter

100 g/½ cup demerara sugar

2 Bramley/McIntosh apples, peeled, cored and roughly chopped

¼ teaspoon ground nutmeg

½ teaspoon ground cinnamon

finely grated zest of 1 unwaxed lemon

1 tablespoon lemon juice

375 g/12 oz. puff pastry dough, thawed if frozen

1 egg yolk mixed with 1 tablespoon milk

baking sheet, lightly dusted with flour

MAKES 6

These are quick to whip up. You can even use a shop-bought spiced apple purée for a cheat's version. If you are lucky enough to know someone who has a Bramley apple tree, you would be doing them a favour to make use of their windfall, so reserve this recipe for the autumn, for times such as these.

Preheat the oven to 200°C (400°F) Gas 6.

Put the butter and 75 g/5 tablespoons of the sugar in a saucepan over medium heat and leave until the butter has melted. Add the apples, nutmeg, cinnamon and lemon zest and juice. Cover with a lid and stir occasionally for 3–4 minutes, until the apple wedges gracefully collapse into a chunky purée. Set aside to cool slightly.

Roll out the pastry on a lightly floured work surface until ½ cm/¼ inch thick. Trim any curvy edges into straight lines, then cut into about 6 x 10-cm/4-inch squares.

Spoon a dollop of the apple purée in the middle of each pastry square.

Brush the edges with egg wash. Fold over one corner so it meets with the other and press gently. Crimp the edges with a fork or your fingers to seal in the filling. Using a sharp knife, slit the top 4 or 5 times to allow the steam to escape and stop the pastry going soggy. Transfer the turnovers to the prepared baking sheet and glaze with egg wash. Sprinkle the remaining sugar over the top. Bake in the preheated oven for 20 minutes, until golden and puffed up.

Let cool for a few moments before devouring (without burning your mouth on the hot filling!), or eat cold.

pancakes & waffles

Potato & rosemary pancakes with bacon & honey Buckwheat crêpes with mushrooms, caramelized onions, bacon & gruyère **Blinis with smoked salmon & crème fraîche** Sweet potato pancakes with hot smoked trout & chilli-lime butter Orange cornmeal hotcakes with orange flower syrup **Blueberry pancakes** Apricot pancakes with maple & pecan butter Lemon ricotta pancakes with blackberries **Buckwheat & banana pancakes** Dairy-free coconut pancakes with lime syrup & mango Buttermilk waffles with crème fraîche, bitter chocolate sauce & hazelnuts **Gingerbread waffles with strawberries**

Potato & rosemary pancakes with bacon & honey

500 g/1 lb. potatoes

1 tablespoon finely chopped
fresh rosemary needles

150 g/1 cup plus 2
tablespoons plain/all-
purpose flour

½ teaspoon bicarbonate
of/baking soda

275 ml/1 cup plus 2
tablespoons buttermilk

12 slices of bacon

2 tablespoons butter

sea salt and freshly ground
black pepper

(clear) honey, to serve

SERVES 4

These pancakes are based on the Irish potato dish called boxty, in which some of the potatoes are cooked and mashed, and the others are grated to give the pancakes a bit of texture on top of the fluffiness. They were obviously once seen as a sign of domesticity, as they prompted the saying: 'Boxty on the griddle, boxty in the pan, if you can't make boxty, you'll never get a man'.

Put a generous half of the potatoes in a saucepan of cold, salted water and bring to the boil. Cook for 20–25 minutes, until soft. Drain and mash, then season and add the rosemary. Let cool.

Meanwhile, peel and grate the remaining potatoes and leave them raw. Put both sets of potato in a mixing bowl and beat in the flour and bicarbonate of/baking soda, then the buttermilk.

Preheat the grill/broiler.

Grill/broil the bacon until well done (there's no need to turn it over while it's being grilled/broiled). Let cool for

4–5 minutes, until crisp. Turn off the grill/broiler and keep the bacon in a low oven while you continue cooking.

Heat half the butter in a frying pan over low/medium heat and wait for it to sizzle. Drop 2–3 ladlefuls of the batter into the pan, spaced apart, and spread out with a spatula. They need about 3 minutes on the first side, then a little less on the other side. Keep warm with the bacon in the oven while you cook the rest.

Serve 2–3 pancakes per person, with a few slices of bacon and some honey to drizzle over.

50 g/⅓ cup buckwheat flour
50 g/½ cup plain/all-
    purpose flour
I large egg
150 ml/⅔ cup whole milk
sunflower oil, for frying
sea salt and freshly ground
    black pepper

FILLING
2 tablespoons butter
2 large red onions, sliced
sprig of fresh thyme
200 g/6½ oz. cremini
    mushrooms, sliced
200 g/6½ oz. (smoked)
    bacon, cubed
2 garlic cloves, sliced
100 g/⅔ cup grated
    Gruyère cheese
150 ml/⅔ cup crème
    fraîche
22-cm/9-in. frying pan
SERVES 4

Buckwheat crêpes with mushrooms, caramelized onions, bacon & gruyère

This is a classic combination from Normandy. Make sure your batter is thin enough to run over the pan easily or you'll end up with crêpes that are not delicate and lacy, but thick and stodgy.

Mix the flours and a large pinch of salt in a mixing bowl and make a well in the middle. Beat the egg and milk in a small bowl, and pour into the flours. Gradually draw the flour into the liquid with a wooden spoon until smooth. Cover and refrigerate for 1 hour.

Preheat the oven to low.

Whisk 80 ml/⅓ cup cold water into the rested batter – it should now be the consistency of single/light cream.

To make the filling, heat the butter in a frying pan over low heat. Stir in the onions and thyme, season with black pepper, cover and cook for 10 minutes,

until the onion has softened. Turn up the heat and add the mushrooms, bacon and garlic. Stir for 6–8 minutes, until lightly caramelized. Stir in the Gruyère and crème fraîche and remove from the heat.

Heat the 22-cm/9-in. frying pan over medium heat. Grease the pan with a kitchen paper/paper towel dipped in oil. Pour in 3 tablespoons of the batter, swirl to coat the base of the pan and cook for 1 minute on each side. Keep warm in the oven while you cook the rest.

Reheat the filling until bubbling and smooth (remove the thyme sprig), season, then divide between the crêpes.

Blinis with smoked salmon & crème fraîche

It's worth making your own fresh blinis because their flavour is much more complex than the ready-made kind. You can make the batter the night before, then let it have its final rising half an hour before cooking. They freeze well too.

50 g/⅓ cup buckwheat
    flour plus 50 g/½ cup
    strong plain/bread flour
I teaspoon salt
125 ml/½ cup whole milk
75 ml/⅓ cup crème
    fraîche, plus extra
7 g/I envelope dried active
    yeast
I large egg, separated
sunflower oil, for frying
smoked salmon, to serve
snipped chives (optional)
MAKES 20 SMALL BLINIS

Sift the flours and salt into a large mixing bowl. Heat the milk in a saucepan until hand hot. Add the crème fraîche and yeast and stir until smooth. Pour onto the flours with the egg yolk and stir well to blend. Cover and let rise for 1 hour.

Beat the egg white with an electric handheld whisk until soft peaks form. Fold into the batter, cover and leave for 30 minutes. Preheat the oven to low.

To make the blinis, heat a heavy-based frying pan over medium heat. Grease with kitchen paper/paper towel dipped in oil. Drop in 2 tablespoons of the batter. After 30 seconds bubbles will appear on the surface. Flip the blini over and cook for 30 seconds on the other side. Keep warm in the oven while you cook the rest. Serve with crème fraîche, smoked salmon, chives, if using, and black pepper.

Blinis with smoked salmon & crème fraîche (left)

Ingredients

250 g/9 oz. sweet potato

3 tablespoons sunflower
oil, plus extra for frying

225 ml/1 cup whole milk

1 egg

130 g/1 cup plain/all-
purpose flour

2 teaspoons baking powder

a pinch of cayenne pepper

2 teaspoons fish sauce

225 g/8 oz. hot smoked
trout

fresh coriander/cilantro,
to garnish

CHILLI-LIME BUTTER

2 spring onions/scallions,
sliced

1 red chilli, shredded

1 teaspoon grated fresh
ginger

1 teaspoon demerara sugar

2 teaspoons fish sauce

juice of 2 limes

75 g/5 tablespoons butter

SERVES 4

Sweet potato pancakes with hot smoked trout & chilli-lime butter

This makes a delicious Thai-inspired brunch dish. The sweet potato helps to keep the pancakes beautifully moist and using fish sauce instead of salt adds another Thai-style touch. The chilli-lime butter soaks into the pancakes and really brings out the flavour of the sweet potato. Even if the dish sounds a little novel to you, try it because all the flavours work beautifully and it makes a change from the usual maple syrup and pancake combination.

Preheat the oven to low.

Peel and halve the sweet potato and put in a saucepan of boiling water. Simmer for 25 minutes until really soft.

Drain the potatoes and mash with the oil. Stir in the milk and let the mixture cool before beating in the egg. Sift in the flour, baking powder and cayenne pepper, and season with the fish sauce. Set aside.

To make the chilli-lime butter, mix the spring onions/scallions, chilli, ginger, sugar, fish sauce and lime juice and set aside.

Heat a frying pan over medium heat.

Grease the pan with kitchen paper/paper towel dipped in oil. Drop in 2 tablespoons of the potato batter and cook for about 2 minutes on the first side, until bubbles appear and the edges are dry. Flip over and cook on the other side for a further 2 minutes. Keep warm in the oven while you cook the rest.

Melt the butter for the chilli-lime butter in a saucepan and stir in the reserved dressing. Serve the pancakes topped with trout and coriander/cilantro and pour over the warm chilli-lime butter.

Orange cornmeal hotcakes with orange flower syrup

150 ml/⅔ cup buttermilk

2 eggs, separated

3 tablespoons orange juice

finely grated zest of
½ orange

50 g/½ cup cornmeal or
polenta

50 g/½ cup plain/all-
purpose flour

3 tablespoons (soft) brown
sugar

1 teaspoon baking powder

a pinch of salt

melted butter, to serve

ORANGE FLOWER SYRUP

120 ml/½ cup maple syrup

a drop of orange flower
water

SERVES 4

These pancakes have a citrusy tang to them and a slightly granular crunch from the cornmeal. The maple syrup is spiked with a small drop of fragrant orange flower water, but a little bit of butter on the hotcakes first won't go amiss.

Preheat the oven to low.

To make the orange flower syrup, stir the maple syrup and orange flower water together in a small bowl.

Put the buttermilk, egg yolks, orange juice and zest in a mixing bowl and beat together. Add the cornmeal, flour, sugar, baking powder and salt and fold in until just moistened. Do not overmix otherwise you will toughen the texture.

Whisk the egg whites in a separate bowl with an electric handheld whisk until soft peaks form. Using a large metal spoon, fold the whites into the batter.

Wipe a frying pan with kitchen paper/paper towel dipped in melted butter. Heat up, then drop in 2–3 tablespoons of the batter. Cook for 2 minutes, until bubbles appear on the top and the edges are dry. Cook in batches of 3 or whatever fits comfortably in your pan. Flip the hotcake over and cook for 2 minutes on the other side.

Serve about 3 hotcakes per person. Put some melted butter on each hotcake and serve with the orange flower syrup.

Blueberry pancakes

125 g/1 cup self-raising
flour

1 teaspoon baking powder

2 tablespoons (caster)
sugar

¼ teaspoon salt

1 egg

100 ml/⅓ cup whole milk

50 g/3 tablespoons butter,
melted

150 g/1 generous cup
blueberries, plus extra

maple syrup, to serve

SERVES 4

Perfect blueberry pancakes should be light and fluffy, with a good rise on them. The secret is to use some water – an all-milk batter makes the pancakes heavier. And remember to serve them with lashings of maple syrup.

Preheat the oven to low.

Sift the flour and baking powder into a large mixing bowl and stir in the sugar and salt. Put the egg, milk and 75 ml/⅓ cup water in another bowl and beat to combine.

Stir half the butter into the wet ingredients in the bowl. Mix the wet ingredients with the dry ingredients until no lumps of flour remain.

Wipe a heavy-based frying pan with scrunched-up kitchen paper/paper towel dipped in the remaining melted butter. Heat up, then drop in 4 tablespoons of the batter. Cook for 1–2 minutes on the first side, then scatter over a few of the blueberries and flip the pancake over. Cook for 2 minutes, until golden and cooked through. Keep warm in the oven while you make the rest.

Serve with more blueberries and lashings of maple syrup.

Blueberry pancakes (left)

Apricot pancakes with maple & pecan butter

125 g/1 cup self-raising
    flour

1 teaspoon baking powder

2 tablespoons (caster) sugar

50 g/3 tablespoons butter,
    melted

¼ teaspoon salt

1 egg

150 ml/⅔ cup whole milk

4 apricots, pitted and
    roughly chopped

MAPLE & PECAN BUTTER

3 tablespoons shelled
    pecans, chopped

75 g/5 tablespoons butter,
    softened

2 tablespoons maple syrup

SERVES 4

Soft stone/drupe fruit works beautifully with fluffy pancakes, but make sure they are really soft and ripe. Apricots are among my favourite fruit, with their sweet perfumed flesh and inoffensively furry skin.

Preheat the oven to low.

To make the maple & pecan butter, put the pecans in a dry frying pan over medium heat and let them heat up. Stir so they brown evenly, then remove from the heat.

Beat the butter and maple syrup together. It may take a while to come together but once it warms up enough it will blend smoothly. Stir in the toasted pecans and set aside.

Sift the flour and baking powder in a large mixing bowl and stir in the sugar and salt. Put half the butter, the egg, milk and 75 ml/⅓ cup water in another bowl and beat to combine. Mix the wet ingredients with the dry ingredients until no lumps of flour remain.

Wipe a heavy-based frying pan with scrunched-up kitchen paper/paper towel dipped in melted butter. Heat up, then drop in 2–3 tablespoons of batter on one side of the pan and the same on the other side of the pan. Cook for about 1–2 minutes on the first side, until the edges look dry, then scatter over some apricots and flip over. Cook for 2 minutes, until golden and cooked through. Keep warm in the oven while you make the rest. Serve with the maple & pecan butter.

Lemon ricotta pancakes with blackberries

250 g/1 cup ricotta

juice and grated zest of
    1 unwaxed lemon

3 eggs, separated

50 g/3 tablespoons butter,
    melted

100 g/¾ cup plain/all-
    purpose flour

1 teaspoon bicarbonate
    of/baking soda

a pinch of salt

4 tablespoons (caster) sugar

blackberries and crème
    fraîche, to serve

SERVES 4

These pancakes are very fluffy and light. They need cooking slowly as they are so delicate. You can turn them into savoury pancakes by omitting the sugar and folding through some chopped green herbs, such as chives and tarragon, then serving with smoked salmon instead of blackberries.

Preheat the oven to low.

Put the ricotta, lemon juice and zest, egg yolks and half the butter in a mixing bowl and beat together. Sift in the flour, bicarbonate of/baking soda and salt and fold in. Whisk the egg whites in a separate bowl with an electric handheld whisk until soft peaks form. Add the sugar and whisk until glossy and firm. Using a large metal spoon, fold the whites into the batter.

Wipe a heavy-based frying pan with scrunched-up kitchen paper/paper towel dipped in the melted butter. Drop a big tablespoon of batter in the pan to make a 6-cm/2½-inch circle. Cook in batches of 3 or 4 depending on the size of the pan. Cook for 2 minutes on each side until risen and cooked through. Keep warm in the oven while you make the rest. Serve with blackberries and crème fraîche.

Lemon ricotta pancakes with blackberries (right)

Buckwheat & banana pancakes

75 g/½ cup buckwheat
   flour
40 g/6 tablespoons plain/
   all-purpose flour
1 teaspoon bicarbonate
   of/baking soda
¼ teaspoon salt
2 tablespoons (clear) honey,
   plus extra to serve
2 eggs, separated
250 ml/1 cup sour cream
sunflower oil, for frying
2 bananas, sliced
SERVES 4

The bananas in these pancakes become caramelized in the hot pan, and when you drizzle over some honey before serving, everything becomes even sweeter.

Preheat the oven to low.

Sift the flours, bicarbonate of/baking soda and salt into a large mixing bowl. Put the honey, egg yolks and sour cream in another bowl and beat to combine. Mix the wet ingredients with the dry ingredients until no lumps of flour remain. Whisk the egg whites in a separate bowl with an electric handheld whisk until soft peaks form. Using a large metal spoon, fold the whites into the batter.

Heat a heavy-based frying pan over medium heat. Grease the pan with a kitchen paper/paper towel dipped in oil. Drop 2–3 tablespoons of batter into the pan. Cook for 1–2 minutes on the first side, until the edges look dry, then scatter over 3–4 slices of banana and flip the pancake over. Cook for 2 minutes, until golden and cooked through. Keep warm in the oven while you make the rest. Serve with honey, for drizzling.

Dairy-free coconut pancakes with lime syrup & mango

150 g/1 cup plus 2
   tablespoons plain/all-
   purpose flour
3 teaspoons baking powder
¼ teaspoon salt
2 tablespoons demerara
   sugar
3 tablespoons desiccated
   coconut
200 ml/¾ cup coconut milk
2 tablespoons sunflower
   oil, plus extra for frying
1 mango, peeled, pitted and
   sliced

LIME SYRUP
juice of 3 limes
grated zest of 1 lime
100 g/½ cup (clear) honey
6 cardamom pods, crushed
SERVES 4

These pancakes are completely dairy free; they don't even contain egg. This makes them a bit more dense but as they are drenched in a runny lime and honey syrup before serving, this is soon taken care of. Try to find the ripest, most perfumed mango to make this dish exquisite.

Preheat the oven to low.

To make the lime syrup, put the lime juice and zest, honey and cardamom pods in a small saucepan and bring to the boil. Boil for 5 minutes, then remove from the heat and set aside.

Meanwhile, sift the flour, baking powder and salt into a large mixing bowl and stir in the sugar and desiccated coconut. Put the coconut milk, 75 ml/ ⅓ cup water and the oil in another bowl

and beat to combine. Mix the wet ingredients with the dry ingredients until no lumps of flour remain.

Heat a heavy-based frying pan over medium heat. Grease the pan with a kitchen paper/paper towel dipped in oil. Drop 2–3 tablespoons of batter into the pan. Cook for 1–2 minutes on each side until golden and cooked through. Keep warm in the oven while you make the rest. Serve with mango and lime syrup.

Dairy-free coconut pancakes with lime syrup & mango (left)

Buttermilk waffles with crème fraîche, bitter chocolate sauce & hazelnuts

150 g/1 cup plus 2
  tablespoons plain/all-
  purpose flour
½ teaspoon bicarbonate
  of/baking soda
1 teaspoon baking powder
3 tablespoons (caster) sugar
2 eggs
1 teaspoon vanilla extract
50 g/3 tablespoons butter,
  melted, plus extra
275 ml/1 big cup buttermilk
3 tablespoons chopped
  hazelnuts
crème fraîche, to serve

BITTER CHOCOLATE
  SAUCE
100 g/3½ oz. dark
  chocolate
1 tablespoon butter
waffle iron
SERVES 4

It is fairly indulgent to go for waffles with chocolate and crème fraîche before you have even ventured out into the world, but now and again, it's good to be decadent! The sauce is so easy and making it with water rather than cream is not a thrifty cheat, but a way of bringing out the bitterness in the chocolate.

Preheat the oven to low.

Sift the flour, bicarbonate of/baking soda and baking powder into a large mixing bowl. Put the sugar, eggs, vanilla extract, butter, buttermilk and 50 ml/ ¼ cup water in another bowl and beat to combine. Pour the wet ingredients into the dry ingredients and whisk until blended. Set aside.

To make the bitter chocolate sauce, put the chocolate, butter and 80 ml/ ⅓ cup water in a heatproof bowl over a saucepan of gently simmering water. Do not let the base of the bowl touch the water. Let melt for 5 minutes. Remove from the heat and stir until smooth. Keep

warm on the pan. Meanwhile, put the hazelnuts in a dry frying pan over medium heat and let them heat up. Stir so they brown evenly, then remove from the heat.

When you're ready to cook the waffles, heat your waffle iron and grease with oil. Ladle in enough batter to fill it, then close. Check the manufacturer's instructions for cooking times, but it should need about 3–5 minutes. When ready, steam will stop escaping from the sides and the waffles will look crisp and golden. Keep warm in the oven while you cook the rest. Serve hot with crème fraîche, a drizzle of chocolate sauce and a scattering of toasted hazelnuts.

Gingerbread waffles with strawberries

150 g/1 cup plus 2
    tablespoons plain/all-
    purpose flour
½ teaspoon bicarbonate
    of/baking soda
1 teaspoon baking powder
1 teaspoon ground
    cinnamon
1 teaspoon ground ginger
⅛ teaspoon ground nutmeg
3 tablespoons molasses
2 eggs
50 g/3 tablespoons butter,
    melted, plus extra
200 ml/¾ cup whole milk
clear honey and
    strawberries, to serve
waffle iron

MAKES 8–12

Depending on the size and shape of your waffle iron, this recipe will make a batch of 8 or much more if your waffle maker makes thin ones. If you don't have such a contraption (not everyone feels the need for a waffle maker in their lives), you can make these into pancakes by simply cooking them in a heavy-based frying pan or on a flat griddle.

Preheat the oven to low.

Sift the flour, bicarbonate of/baking soda, baking powder and spices in a large mixing bowl. Put the molasses, eggs, butter and milk in another bowl and beat to combine. Pour the wet ingredients into the dry ingredients and beat to combine. Don't worry about any small lumps.

Heat your waffle iron and grease with oil. Ladle in enough batter to fill it, then close. Check the manufacturer's instructions for cooking times, but it should need about 3–5 minutes. When ready, steam will stop escaping from the sides and the waffles will look crisp and golden. Keep warm in the oven while you cook the rest. Serve hot with honey and a handful of the sweetest strawberries.

mains

Baked tomatoes stuffed with goat cheese & herbs Pancetta, taleggio, roasted leek & onion tart **Cheesy polenta with sausages & red onions** **English breakfast quiche** Courgette/zucchini fritters with tomato & feta salad Garlic mushrooms & goat cheese on sourdough toast **Corn cakes with bacon & avocado** Crab cakes with slaw & sweet chilli sauce Hot smoked salmon hash with dill crème fraîche **Sweet potato, chorizo & fried egg hash** Dukkah & harissa sausage rolls Smoked haddock kedgeree **Linguine with lemon, basil & parmesan cream**

Baked tomatoes stuffed with goat cheese & herbs

4 large, stuffing tomatoes
such as Marmande or
heirloom, or more of
a smaller variety

2 tablespoons extra virgin
olive oil, plus extra
to drizzle

1 onion, finely chopped

1 tablespoon chopped
fresh thyme leaves

200 g/6½ oz. goat cheese

4 tablespoons dried
breadcrumbs

2 eggs, beaten

a handful of fresh basil
leaves

SERVES 4

Stuffed tomatoes are quite an old-fashioned idea, but I was reminded just how delectable they can be on a recent trip to France. When you see the quirky-looking shapes of the Marmande and heirloom tomatoes in their various shades of green and orange, that's the time to make this dish. The secret is to slightly undercook them so the tomatoes don't just collapse into amoeba-like blobs. I like to use quite a strong aged goat cheese for this, as it contrasts against the sweetness of the tomatoes when they are cooked.

Preheat the oven to 180°C (350°F) Gas 4.

Slice the top third off the tomatoes and reserve. Using a melon baller, scoop out the seeds and juices and discard or reserve for making a tomato sauce.

Heat the oil in a frying pan, add the onion and thyme and soften for 5 minutes. Let cool slightly.

In a mixing bowl, beat the goat cheese, breadcrumbs and eggs together and season well. Stir in the onion mixture and a few of the basil leaves. Divide the stuffing between the hollow tomatoes and top with the reserved tomato hats. Arrange in a baking dish, drizzle with oil and scatter over the remaining basil leaves. Bake in the preheated oven for 18–20 minutes.

Pancetta, taleggio, roasted leek & onion tart

2 leeks, thickly sliced

2 red onions, peeled and
cut into slim wedges

2 tablespoons extra virgin
olive oil, plus extra
to drizzle

1 tablespoon balsamic
vinegar

375 g/12 oz. ready-rolled
puff pastry dough,
thawed if frozen

150 g/5 oz. Taleggio (rind
removed), cubed

8 wafer-thin slices of
pancetta

2 handfuls of rocket/arugula

sea salt and freshly ground
black pepper

SERVES 4–6

Roasted leeks are one of my favourite ways with vegetables. I love that they are sweet and crispy at the same time. They go brilliantly atop a tart, needing only creamy cheese to finish them off. I have used the soft, slightly stinky Taleggio in this version, but you could just as easily use a blue cheese or mozzarella.

Preheat the oven to 200°C (400°F) Gas 6.

Put the leeks, onions, oil and balsamic vinegar in a roasting tray and season. Toss well, then roast in the preheated oven for 30–35 minutes, until soft. Leave the oven on for the tart.

Meanwhile, unroll the ready-rolled puff pastry, lay it on a baking sheet and prick all over with a fork.

When the roasting vegetables are soft and slightly charred, scatter them evenly over the pastry. Drop the cubed Taleggio all over, then drape the pancetta slices over everything. Bake in the oven for 25–30 minutes until the pastry is golden and well risen at the edges. Strew the rocket/arugula over the top and drizzle with a little extra olive oil before serving.

Cheesy polenta with sausages & red onions

12 pork sausages

2 red onions, peeled and
cut into slim wedges

a handful of fresh
sage leaves

6 tablespoons olive oil

150 g/1 cup instant polenta

1 tablespoon chopped
fresh thyme leaves

50 g/½ cup grated
Parmesan

200 g/1⅓ cups crumbled
feta

sea salt and freshly ground
black pepper

*20-cm/8-in. square pan,
greased*

SERVES 4

If you are not yet sold on polenta, I urge you to try this method of preparation because it has converted many a person. The secret is that it needs to be seasoned well and enriched with lots of cheese, as well as being fried over high heat until golden so that you get the crunchy exterior and the soft creaminess inside.

Preheat the oven to 190°C (375°F) Gas 5.

Put the sausages and onions in a roasting pan. Scatter the sage over the top and drizzle with 2 tablespoons of the oil, then toss everything together. Roast in the preheated oven for 30–35 minutes, until golden and cooked through.

Bring 650 ml/2⅔ cups water to the boil with a pinch of salt and 1 tablespoon of the oil. Remove from the heat and pour in the polenta. Mix it with a wooden spoon and lots of elbow grease. Return to low heat for about 2–3 minutes,

stirring constantly. Remove from the heat, beat in the thyme and cheeses and season generously. Spoon into the prepared pan and smooth out the surface. Let cool and set.

Tip the polenta onto a board and quarter, then cut each quarter in half to make triangles.

Heat a frying pan over high heat and add the remaining oil. Add as many polenta triangles as you can and fry for 2–3 minutes on each side, until golden. Serve with the sausage mixture.

Cheesy polenta with sausages & red onions (left)

PASTRY

225 g/1¾ cups plain/all-
  purpose flour

1 teaspoon English
  mustard powder

150 g/10 tablespoons
  butter, chilled and cubed

1 egg, beaten

FILLING

4 pork sausages

200 g/6½ oz. cherry
  tomatoes, halved

200 g/6½ oz. bacon, cubed

200 g/6½ oz. button
  mushrooms, halved

1 tablespoon olive oil

300 ml/1¼ cups crème
  fraîche

3 large eggs, beaten

1 teaspoon English
  mustard powder

*25-cm/10-in. fluted, loose-
  bottomed tart pan*

baking beans

SERVES 6

English breakfast quiche

Here are all the flavours of a traditional full farmhouse English fry-up in a quiche. Bake it the day before a long, early-morning journey when you have to have your breakfast on the go. Try to resist smothering it in ketchup!

Preheat the oven to 200°C (400°F) Gas 6.

To make the pastry, put the flour, mustard powder and butter in a food processor and pulse until they are just combined. Add the egg and run the motor until the mixture just comes into a ball. Turn out, wrap with clingfilm/plastic wrap and refrigerate for 30 minutes.

To make the filling, put the sausages in a roasting pan and roast in the preheated oven for 10 minutes. Take the pan out of the oven, throw in the tomatoes, bacon and mushrooms, drizzle over the oil and return to the oven to roast for 15–20 minutes, until everything is tender and cooked through. Leave the oven on.

Roll out the pastry on a lightly floured surface until it is about 3 mm/⅛ inch thick and use to line the tart pan. Press the

pastry into the corners and leave the overhang. Prick the base with a fork, line with baking parchment and fill with baking beans. Bake in the oven for 8 minutes, then remove the beans and paper. Trim off the overhang and reduce the heat to 150°C (300°F) Gas 2. Return the pastry case to the oven for 2–3 minutes to dry out while you prepare the filling.

To finish the filling, slice the sausages and scatter them with the rest of the roasted ingredients into the pastry case. Mix the crème fraîche, eggs and mustard powder and pour over everything in the pastry case. Bake for 30–35 minutes, until set around the edges. Turn off the oven and let the tart cool in the oven, with the door open, for 15 minutes. Cut into slices and serve warm or cold.

Courgette/zucchini fritters with tomato & feta salad

3 courgettes/zucchini, grated

½ red onion, finely chopped

1 teaspoon cumin seeds

2 red chillies, finely chopped

75 g/⅔ cup plain/all-
purpose flour

½ teaspoon bicarbonate
of/baking soda

2 tablespoons fresh mint
leaves, chopped

2 eggs, beaten

4 tablespoons olive oil

TOMATO & FETA SALAD

1 tablespoon red wine
vinegar

½ teaspoon English
mustard powder

3 tablespoons olive oil

3 tomatoes, chopped

4 spring onions/scallions,
sliced

200 g/1⅓ cups crumbled
feta

SERVES 4

These little fritters are a great way of using up courgettes/zucchini if you have a glut of them in your garden. The courgettes/zucchini are salted in order to remove some of the moisture (not the bitterness), otherwise they can be quite soggy. You can serve the fritters with this tomato & feta salad or just a simple yogurt and mint dip, if you prefer.

Preheat the oven to low.

Put the courgettes/zucchini and a good pinch of salt in a colander. Toss well to distribute the salt and leave for 20 minutes. Squeeze the courgettes/zucchini to extract some moisture, then pat dry with kitchen paper/paper towels.

Mix the courgettes/zucchini with the onion, cumin seeds, chillies, flour, bicarbonate of/baking soda, mint and eggs in a mixing bowl. The mixture will seem quite dry at first but the courgettes/zucchini will moisten everything the more you stir. Season and leave for 10 minutes.

To make the tomato & feta salad, whisk together the vinegar and mustard powder, then add the oil and whisk until it emulsifies. Season. Mix the tomatoes, spring onions/scallions, feta and dressing.

Heat the oil in a nonstick frying pan over medium/high heat. Drop a big tablespoon of batter into the pan. Cook in batches of 3–4 depending on the size of the pan. Cook for 2–3 minutes on each side, until really golden and cooked through. Keep warm in the oven while you cook the rest. Serve with a mound of the tomato & feta salad.

Garlic mushrooms & goat cheese on sourdough toast

8 field mushrooms

3 garlic cloves, crushed

3 tablespoons olive oil

3 tablespoons pine nuts

2 tablespoons balsamic
vinegar

4 slices of sourdough bread

150 g/5 oz. fresh goat cheese

fresh tarragon, to serve

sea salt and freshly
ground black pepper

SERVES 4

Garlicky mushrooms are great for breakfast, but try them on a layer of soft, creamy goat cheese and you will be in utter heaven. The kind of cheese you are looking for is a soft fresh cheese, not aged, so it will not have a rind. You could also use ricotta if you like. Seek out a good, sturdy rustic bread such as sourdough for this dish to prevent the underneath going soggy.

Preheat the oven to 200°C (400°F) Gas 6.

Put the mushrooms, garlic and oil in a roasting pan. Toss well and season. Roast in the preheated oven for 15 minutes, until tender. Stir in the pine nuts and balsamic vinegar halfway through roasting.

Just before the mushrooms are ready, toast the slices of sourdough bread and spread with the goat cheese. Place the mushrooms on top, stalk side up, scatter with the tarragon and serve immediately. Add more seasoning, if necessary.

Garlic mushrooms & goat cheese on sourdough toast (left)

Corn cakes with bacon & avocado

75 g/²/₃ cup self-raising flour

30 g/¼ cup cornmeal or polenta

½ teaspoon bicarbonate of/baking soda

a pinch of cayenne pepper

2 large eggs

150 ml/²/₃ cup sour cream

400 g/14 oz. drained canned corn

3 spring onions/scallions, sliced

12 slices of bacon

sunflower oil, for frying

1 avocado, pitted and sliced

a handful of rocket/arugula

sea salt and freshly ground black pepper

SERVES 4

If you are veering towards lunch rather than breakfast, you could serve this with a mound of baby spinach and rocket/arugula dressed in lemon and olive oil and perhaps a few roasted peppers to make it more substantial.

Preheat the grill/broiler.

Put the flour, cornmeal, bicarbonate of/baking soda and cayenne pepper in a mixing bowl. In a separate bowl, whisk together the eggs, sour cream, corn and spring onions/scallions. Pour this into the dry ingredients, season and mix until blended. The batter should be fairly firm.

Grill/broil the bacon until really crisp.

Heat 2 tablespoons oil in a frying pan over medium heat. Drop 2 tablespoons of batter into the pan and cook in batches of about 3, depending on the size of the pan. Cook the corn cakes for 2 minutes on each side, until golden brown and cooked through. Transfer to a plate and cover with foil to keep warm while you cook the rest.

Serve the corn cakes with a few slices of avocado, the crisp bacon and a couple of rocket/arugula leaves. Grind over some black pepper.

Crab cakes with slaw & sweet chilli sauce

500 g/1 lb. cooked crabmeat

50 g/½ cup dried breadcrumbs

1 egg, beaten

3 tablespoons mayonnaise

¼ teaspoon cayenne pepper

3 tablespoons chopped fresh coriander/cilantro

4 tablespoons olive oil

sea salt and freshly ground black pepper

sweet chilli sauce, to serve

SLAW

1 apple, peeled

2 carrots

½ small red cabbage

6 spring onions/scallions

juice of 1 lime

4 tablespoons mayonnaise

1 garlic clove, crushed

SERVES 4

Crab cakes are not cheap to make so it's a good choice when you have people coming over for more of a fancy lunchy brunch. Canned crabmeat or a dressed crab will work, but if you do use dressed crab, omit the extra mayonnaise as it usually has some mayo already mixed in.

Put the crabmeat, breadcrumbs, egg, mayonnaise, cayenne pepper and coriander/cilantro in a large mixing bowl, season and mix until blended. Shape the mixture into 8 x 8-cm/3-inch patties and lay on a sheet of greaseproof paper on a baking sheet. Refrigerate for 1 hour.

Preheat the oven to low.

To make the slaw, feed the apple and carrots through the grater on your food processor, or do it by hand if you don't have one. Shred the cabbage by hand as thinly as you can, or use the slicing attachment on the food processor. Thinly slice the spring onions/scallions. Tip everything into a large bowl. Add the lime juice, mayonnaise and garlic and stir well. Set aside while you finish the crab cakes.

Heat the oil in a large frying pan over high heat. Fry the crab cakes in batches (keeping them warm in the oven as you go) for 3–4 minutes on each side, until crisp and deep golden.

Spoon a mound of slaw onto each plate and serve 2 crab cakes on top. Serve with sweet chilli sauce.

Corn cakes with bacon & avocado (right)

Hot smoked salmon hash with dill crème fraîche

500 g/1 lb. new potatoes,
  halved

4 tablespoons olive oil

2 onions, sliced

150 g/5 oz. (streaky) bacon,
  chopped

1 tablespoon butter

2 teaspoons capers

200 g/6½ oz. hot smoked
  salmon, broken into
  large chunks

150 g/⅔ cup crème fraîche

juice and grated zest of
  1 lime

1 tablespoon chopped
  fresh dill

sea salt and freshly ground
  black pepper

SERVES 4

Unlike the regular smoked salmon we know so well, hot smoked salmon looks cooked and flakes into beautiful chunks. Mixing it with bacon works really well as they share the same smokiness. A dollop of crème fraîche infused with lime and dill adds a bit of well-needed freshness too.

Put a saucepan of water over medium heat and bring to the boil. Add a pinch of salt and the potatoes. Reduce the heat and let it simmer for 12–15 minutes, until the potatoes are tender.

Meanwhile, put half the oil, the onions and bacon in a frying pan. Cover and cook over low heat for 8–10 minutes, stirring occasionally, until softening. Remove the lid, turn up the heat slightly and cook for 3–4 minutes until slightly golden. Tip onto a plate and set aside.

Drain the potatoes and add the butter and remaining oil to the frying pan you just used for the onion mixture. Add the potatoes and cook over high heat for 5–6 minutes, until browning on all sides. Stir in the onion mixture, capers and salmon and cook for 3–4 minutes, until everything is sizzling and hot, then season.

Mix the crème fraîche, lime zest and enough juice to make it limey but not too runny. Stir in the dill and season. Serve the hash with a dollop of the crème fraîche.

Sweet potato, chorizo & fried egg hash

3 sweet potatoes,
  peeled and cubed

2 red onions, peeled and
  cut into wedges

1 red chilli, sliced

1 teaspoon cumin seeds

4 tablespoons extra virgin
  olive oil

150 g/5 oz. chorizo, sliced

200 g/6½ oz. cherry
  tomatoes, halved

4 eggs

a handful of fresh flat-leaf
  parsley leaves, chopped

sea salt and freshly ground
  black pepper

SERVES 4

This is full of sweet, smoky flavours. I adore vibrant orange sweet potatoes for their unusual starchy taste and I find that anything containing chorizo quickly becomes a firm favourite in our home. Add a fried egg and you can't go wrong!

Preheat the oven to 180°C (350°F) Gas 4.

Put the potatoes, onions, chilli, cumin seeds and half the oil in a roasting pan and toss well. Roast in the preheated oven for 15 minutes. Remove the pan from the oven, throw in the chorizo and tomatoes and return to the oven for 20 minutes, until everything is tender and slightly charred.

Heat the remaining oil in a frying pan over high heat, then crack an egg in each corner and turn the heat right down. Cook for 2–3 minutes until the white has set. If you need to firm up the white, cover with the lid for 30 seconds.

Season the hash and stir in the parsley. Serve each portion of hash with a fried egg on top.

Hot smoked salmon hash with dill crème fraîche (left)

Dukkah & harissa sausage rolls

500 g/1 lb. minced/ground
lamb

1 teaspoon smoked
paprika

1 teaspoon ground
cinnamon

4 tablespoons harissa or
sun-dried tomato paste

500 g/1 lb. ready-made
puff pastry dough,
thawed if frozen

1 egg, beaten

sea salt and freshly ground
black pepper

DUKKAH

2 tablespoons sesame
seeds

2 tablespoons pine nuts

1 teaspoon coriander
seeds

1 teaspoon cumin seeds

baking sheet, lightly oiled

SERVES 4

The plain old sausage roll gets a bit of an exotic makeover here. When I realized that most people like to drench their sausage rolls in tomato ketchup I thought, why not add some tomato to the meat. Hopefully this is enough to prevent my rolls from the ketchup fate. Not only have I used lamb, not pork, for the filling, but I have also spiced it with cinnamon and smoked paprika. And the top is speckled with an Egyptian spice blend called dukkah. This blend varies from recipe to recipe, so feel free to use up any remnants of nuts or seeds that you have.

Preheat the oven to 200°C (400°F) Gas 6.

To make the dukkah, put the sesame seeds, pine nuts, coriander seeds, cumin seeds and a pinch of salt in a mortar. Bash them with the pestle until crushed, but try to maintain a little texture so they are not pounded into a powder.

Put the lamb, paprika, cinnamon and harissa in a mixing bowl with some seasoning and mix with your hands, squelching it all together until thoroughly blended together.

Roll out the pastry on a lightly floured work surface until you have a rectangle 25 × 60 cm/10 × 24 inches (and about 3 mm/⅛ inch thick). Cut into 4, at 15-cm/6-inch intervals. This will give you 4 rectangles, each 25 × 15 cm/10 × 6 inches. Spoon about 4 tablespoons of the sausage mixture onto each rectangle. Brush a little beaten egg along one short side. Fold the pastry over from one short side to meet the other short side. Press the folded edges together to seal and crimp by pressing down with a fork. Leave the other 2 sides of the rolls open so that you can still see the filling.

Repeat to make 3 more rolls. Brush them with more beaten egg and sprinkle the dukkah over the top.

Transfer to the prepared baking sheet and bake in the preheated oven for about 25–35 minutes, until golden and cooked through.

Smoked haddock kedgeree

50 g/3 tablespoons butter

2 onions, thinly sliced

4 eggs

1 teaspoon ground cumin

1 teaspoon ground
coriander

1/2 teaspoon ground
turmeric

175 g/3/4 cup plus 2
tablespoons basmati rice

300 ml/1 1/4 cups boiling
water

400 g/14 oz. smoked
haddock

juice of 1 lemon

a handful of fresh curly
parsley leaves, chopped

SERVES 4

Kedgeree is an old English dish left over from the Victorian days when, in a flurry of Anglo-Indian mania, it graced breakfast tables around the land. It developed from a simple Indian dish of rice and lentils called khichari.

Bring a small saucepan of water to the boil for the eggs. Meanwhile, melt the butter in a casserole dish over low heat, add the onions and stir to coat in the butter. Cook, covered, for 10 minutes, stirring occasionally, until soft. Put the eggs in the pan of boiling water and turn it down to a gentle simmer. Simmer for 8 minutes. Drain and run them under cold water. Take the lid off the onions, add the spices and turn up the heat. Cook, stirring, for 3–4 minutes, until the onions are golden brown. Add the rice, stir and pour in the 300 ml/1 1/4 cups boiling water. Cover and turn the heat down so it gently simmers for 8 minutes.

Put the haddock in a frying pan and cover with boiling water. Simmer gently for 5–6 minutes, until cooked though, then drain. Turn off the heat under the rice, keep covered and let steam for 10 minutes. Peel and halve the eggs. Drain the fish and remove the skin and any bones. Flake into chunks and stir into the rice with the lemon juice and parsley. Serve topped with the boiled eggs.

Linguine with lemon, basil & parmesan cream

2 tablespoons butter

2 shallots, finely chopped

1 unwaxed lemon

300 ml/1 1/4 cups whipping
cream

200 ml/3/4 cup hot chicken
or vegetable stock

2 handfuls of fresh basil
leaves, plus more to
serve

350 g/12 oz. dried linguine

75 g/2 1/2 oz. Parmesan or
Pecorino shavings, plus
extra to serve

sea salt and freshly ground
black pepper

SERVES 4

I'm not suggesting you have pasta for breakfast, but if your brunch is a late one, this is an easy dish to whip up. I sometimes add a splash of vodka to the shallots too, which just gives it a slight acidic edge, as wine does. Make sure you go for unwaxed lemons so you are not ingesting all the horrid chemicals on waxed ones.

Heat the butter in a frying pan and add the shallots. Add a pinch of salt, cover and cook over low heat for 6–7 minutes, stirring every now and then, until soft and glossy.

Put a large saucepan of water on to boil for the pasta. Meanwhile, take a potato peeler and pare off the zest of the lemon, leaving behind the white pith. Try to pare the zest in one long piece so you can easily remove it later.

Add the cream, stock, lemon zest and basil to the shallots and gently simmer for 10–15 minutes, uncovered, until it has reduced and thickened – it should only just coat the back of a spoon. Cook the linguine in the boiling water until al dente.

Season the sauce with a little salt and lots of pepper. Fish out the lemon zest. Drain the pasta and return to the pan. Stir in the Parmesan and squeeze in some juice from the lemon. Add more juice or seasoning, to taste. Garnish with more basil and Parmesan shavings.

Linguine with lemon, basil & parmesan cream (left)

sandwiches, salads & sides

Steak & fried egg sandwiches with mustard butter Hot chorizo, avocado & lime sandwiches **Gravadlax with pickles on rye bread** Reubens with beef, sauerkraut & emmenthal Spiced omelette sandwiches with tomato & chilli jam **Quinoa salad with smoked chicken, avocado, pea shoots & toasted almonds** Red rice, dried cherry & pistachio salad with halloumi Pickled herring, beetroot/beet, fennel & chicory/belgian endive salad with yogurt dressing **Hash browns** Bacon & onion rösti Baked beans with maple syrup & paprika **Bacon rolls with chilli & pecans** Roasted balsamic tomatoes

Steak & fried egg sandwiches with mustard butter

100 g/7 tablespoons butter, soft

2 teaspoons wholegrain mustard

½ teaspoon English mustard powder

1 tablespoon chopped fresh tarragon leaves

1 teaspoon Gentleman's relish or anchovy paste (optional)

2 white buns, halved horizontally

2 x 250-g/8-oz. rib-eye or sirloin steaks, roughly 1.5 cm/⅝ inch thick

3 tablespoons olive oil

2 large eggs

sea salt and freshly ground black pepper

SERVES 2

A well-cooked steak with a rosy interior and charred exterior truly is a wonderful thing. I like to adorn it with a butter spiked with the piquant flavour of mustard and tarragon. When the steak is ready, it is clamped in a soft white bap slathered in this delicious butter, which will melt with the steak's residual heat. Along with a fried egg cooked so it is only just runny inside, this is one sandwich that you need to eat fast before the egg and butter have time to trickle down your chin.

Put the butter in a mixing bowl and beat it with a spoon until squished against the sides of the bowl. Spoon in the wholegrain mustard, mustard powder, tarragon and relish, if using. Season to taste, taking care not to over-season as the relish will already be salty. Beat everything together and use to butter the insides of the buns.

Heat a ridged stovetop grill pan over high heat until very hot. Brush the steaks with 1 tablespoon of the oil and season. Using tongs, lay the steaks on the pan and press down. Let them cook for

2–4 minutes on each side. Press the middle of the steak to determine how well cooked it is. A light yield means it is medium, while anything soft is still rare. Transfer the steaks to a board and cut off any large pieces of fat. Let rest for 2–3 minutes while you cook the eggs.

Add the remaining oil to a frying pan and heat over high heat. Crack in the eggs and turn the heat to low. Cook for 2 minutes, then flip over for 30 seconds to cook the other side, but leave the yolk with a bit of ooze. Place a steak in each bun and finish off with a fried egg.

Hot chorizo, avocado & lime sandwiches

1 avocado

juice of ½ lime

110 g/4 oz. chorizo, sliced diagonally

4 slices of country-style bread

a handful of rocket/arugula

sea salt and freshly ground black pepper

SERVES 2

A good nutty avocado is hard to beat. All it needs is some lime juice to perk up the natural flavours. Pair it with sweet, spicy chorizo and you instantly have the perfect sandwich.

Halve the avocado and remove the stone/pit. Using a spoon, scoop out the flesh and mash in a bowl with the lime juice and some seasoning. Set aside.

Heat a frying pan over high heat, then add the chorizo. Fry for 1 minute on each

side, or until crisp and lightly browned. Remove from the heat.

Toast the bread and spread the avocado over 2 slices. Top with the chorizo and rocket/arugula and sandwich with the other piece of toast.

Steak & fried egg sandwiches with mustard butter (right)

Gravadlax with pickles on rye bread

buttered dark rye bread,
to serve

GRAVADLAX

1 tablespoon juniper
berries

1 tablespoon fennel seeds

1 tablespoon black
peppercorns

50 g/¼ cup coarse sea salt

4 tablespoons demerara
sugar

750 g/1½ lbs. salmon fillet,
2–3 cm/1 in. thick, pin
boned and scaled

PICKLES

2 cucumbers, sliced
5 mm/¼ in. thick

1 small onion, thinly sliced

2 tablespoons sea salt

¼ teaspoon celery seeds

1 teaspoon mustard seeds

2 tablespoons prepared
horseradish

5 whole cloves

250 ml/1 cup white wine
vinegar

200 g/1 cup granulated
sugar

SERVES 6–8

I like to make this for a brunch party as it feeds many unexpected guests without any extra effort. Making both the pickles and gravadlax is mainly an assault on your dry stores, so don't be put off by the lengthy list of ingredients. Refrigerated pickles will keep for up to 1 month, which is why the recipe makes a lot more than you can eat in one sitting. The gravadlax is very easy although it does need to be thought about a few days earlier, but once it is done you can forget about it. Make sure you start with the freshest fish as it is ultimately eaten cured but raw.

To make the pickles, put the cucumbers, onion and salt in a large nonmetal bowl. Cover and refrigerate for 2 hours.

Rinse and drain well. Transfer to a medium container. In a small saucepan, heat the celery seeds, mustard seeds, horseradish, cloves, vinegar and sugar. Bring to the boil, to dissolve the sugar, then pour onto the container with the cucumbers. Cover and refrigerate for 1 day to develop a full flavour.

To make the gravadlax, pound the juniper berries, fennel seeds, peppercorns, 1 tablespoon of the salt and the sugar with a pestle and mortar until roughly crushed and aromatic.

Line a nonmetal tray with clingfilm/plastic wrap, leaving enough overlapping to wrap around the salmon later. Scatter one-quarter of the ground spices over the clingfilm/plastic wrap and lay the salmon, skin side down, on top. Cover with the rest of the ground spices. Wrap tightly in the clingfilm/plastic wrap so you form a watertight parcel and weight down with cans of food or a heavy board. Let cure for 12 hours or overnight in the fridge.

Flip the fish over, weight down again and cure for another 12 hours and continue to cure and flip until the fish has had 48 hours.

Unwrap the fish and drain off any juices. Place on a board, skin side down. Slice the gravadlax thinly with a sharp knife, cutting the flesh away from the skin (discard the skin). Serve with buttered rye bread and pickles.

Reubens with beef, sauerkraut & emmenthal

4 tablespoons mayonnaise

3 spring onions/scallions, sliced

2 gherkins, chopped

¼ teaspoon hot horseradish sauce

a dash of Worcestershire sauce

a pinch of (caster) sugar

8 slices of rye bread

300 g/10 oz. corned or salt beef, sliced

200 g/1 cup sauerkraut, drained

100 g/3½ oz. Emmenthal, sliced

SERVES 4

This is a classic American sandwich which contains corned beef (or salt beef), thousand island dressing, sauerkraut and melted Swiss cheese. I am not a huge fan of the dressing so I have tweaked mine slightly.

Put the mayonnaise, spring onions/scallions, gherkins, horseradish and Worcestershire sauces and sugar in a bowl, mix well and set aside.

Preheat the grill/broiler.

Grill/broil the bread for 1–2 minutes on one side, until golden. Remove from the oven and spread dressing over the untoasted side of half the slices. Lay the Emmenthal on the rest and grill/broil for 2–3 minutes to melt.

Meanwhile, put the corned beef, then some sauerkraut over the mayonnaise-covered bread slices. Once the cheese has melted, make up the sandwiches and serve immediately.

Spiced omelette sandwiches with tomato & chilli jam

8 large eggs

1 teaspoon ground cumin

a handful of fresh coriander/cilantro, chopped

2 tablespoons olive oil

1 long baguette

80 g/2½ oz. lamb's lettuce/corn salad

sea salt and freshly ground black pepper

TOMATO & CHILLI JAM

250 g/8 oz. tomatoes

3 red chillies

1 red onion, chopped

3 garlic cloves, sliced

1 cm/½ in. fresh ginger, grated

4 tablespoons red wine vinegar

250 g/1¼ cups demerara sugar

2 tablespoons fish sauce

SERVES 4

The tomato & chilli jam for these sandwiches is made in the oven. Watch it doesn't get too sticky as it will set and harden more on cooling, a bit like jam does. It makes a jarful but you can use it up on other dishes, as it will keep for a month in the fridge. I like using the extra with grilled fish and a dollop of sour cream.

Preheat the oven to 200°C (400°F) Gas 6.

To make the tomato & chilli jam, chop the tomatoes. Remove the seeds from 2 of the chillies but keep the seeds in the third. Chop all the chillies. Put the tomatoes, chillies, onion, garlic, ginger, vinegar and sugar in a roasting tray. Season with fish sauce, stir to combine and roast in the preheated oven for 30–40 minutes, until the tomatoes and onion are well cooked and caramelized. The jam will still be runny but will thicken as it cools. Let cool slightly.

Beat together the eggs, cumin and coriander/cilantro and season. Heat a frying pan (about 20 cm/8 inches in diameter), add the oil and swirl to coat the base of the pan. Pour in half the egg mixture and draw the cooked edges into the middle. Tilt the pan so the uncooked egg runs into the edges. When the omelette is evenly set except for a little unset egg, it is done. Fold it in half and slide it out of the pan onto a board. Cook the remaining egg mixture in the same way.

Slice the baguette horizontally. Slice each omelette in half and stuff into the baguette. Smear with tomato & chilli jam (lots if everyone likes the heat) and add a tangle of lamb's lettuce/corn salad. Cut the baguette into 4 portions and serve.

Reubens with beef, sauerkraut & emmenthal (right)

Quinoa salad with smoked chicken, avocado, pea shoots & toasted almonds

250 g/1 2/3 cups quinoa

75 g/1/2 cup shelled Marcona almonds, chopped

6 tablespoons extra virgin olive oil

3 tablespoons sherry vinegar

1 garlic clove, crushed

300 g/10 oz. smoked chicken, chopped

2 avocados, pitted and chopped

150 g/1 cup cherry tomatoes, halved

a handful of pea shoots

sea salt and freshly ground black pepper

SERVES 4

Quinoa is a grain with a very high protein content. It has a slightly frog spawn look about it, but it tastes like a nutty couscous or bulgur wheat. I adore pea shoots, which seem to be the ingredient *de rigueur*; they taste of peas but have the texture of a soft leaf. Along with smoky chicken and creamy avocado this makes a really gorgeous warm salad for a sunny mid-morning.

Soak the quinoa in a bowl of cold water for 20 minutes.

Meanwhile, put the almonds in a dry frying pan over medium heat and let them heat up. Stir so they brown evenly, then remove from the heat.

Bring a pan of 600 ml/2 1/2 cups water to the boil and when the quinoa has had its time, drain and pour into the boiling water. Cook for 15 minutes.

Make a dressing by whisking together the oil, vinegar, garlic and some seasoning.

Put the chicken, avocados, tomatoes and toasted almonds in a large serving dish. When the quinoa is ready, drain it well and run it under cold water to stop it cooking. Drain again and tip into the dish with the vegetables. Add the dressing and toss together until blended. Gently fold in the pea shoots and serve.

Red rice, dried cherry & pistachio salad with halloumi

250 g/1 1/4 cups Camargue red rice

100 g/2/3 cup dried sour cherries

4 tablespoons extra virgin olive oil

1 tablespoon red wine vinegar

1 garlic clove, crushed

50 g/1/3 cup shelled pistachios

6 spring onions/scallions

250 g/8 oz. halloumi, sliced

2 tablespoons chopped fresh mint

4 tablespoons chopped fresh flat-leaf parsley

sea salt and freshly ground black pepper

SERVES 4

The red rice from the Camargue region of France has a nutty texture. It needs a punchy dressing to wake it up so I have added a crushed garlic clove to a regular vinaigrette. Look out for dried sour cherries for this vibrant salad, but you can use dried cranberries or raisins as a fallback.

Bring a medium saucepan of water to the boil and add the rice. Add a pinch of salt and simmer for 25–30 minutes, until the rice is tender but still has a bite to it.

Meanwhile, soak the cherries in 100 ml/1/2 cup warm water, until they become really plump.

Make a dressing by whisking together 3 tablespoons of the oil, the vinegar and garlic and some seasoning. Drain the cherries and put in a large serving dish with the pistachios. Slice the spring onions/scallions and add those to the serving dish too.

Heat a ridged stovetop grill pan over high heat. Brush the halloumi with the remaining oil and cook for 1–2 minutes on each side, until branded with deep golden lines.

Drain the rice very well and add to the ingredients in the serving dish. Add the dressing and herbs and toss everything together until blended. Spoon onto plates and top with the halloumi.

Red rice, dried cherry & pistachio salad with halloumi (left)

Pickled herring, beetroot/beet, fennel & chicory/belgian endive salad with yogurt dressing

Pickled herring, or roll mops as they are sometimes known, are great in the morning as they are zingy and sweet. Mixed with slivers of fennel and a few bitter chicory/Belgian endive leaves, they make for a very refined salad.

3–4 tablespoons olive oil

juice of 1 lemon

1 fennel, trimmed and
   thinly sliced

sprig of fresh dill, chopped

250 g/8 oz. cooked or raw
   baby beetroot/beets

100 g/½ cup Greek yogurt

1 tablespoon red wine
   vinegar

2 heads of chicory/Belgian
   endive, sliced

280 g/9 oz. pickled herring,
   cubed

sea salt and freshly ground
   black pepper

SERVES 4

Mix together 3 tablespoons of the oil and the lemon juice, then put half of it into a large mixing bowl with the fennel and dill. Season well, toss together and set aside for 1 hour to soften the fennel.

If you need to cook the beetroot/beets, preheat the oven to 200°C (400°F) Gas 6.

To cook the beetroot/beets, scrub them, then put them in a small roasting pan with the remaining oil and some seasoning. Cover with foil and roast in the preheated oven for 25–30 minutes, until tender. Cut this, or your pre-cooked beetroot/beets, into quarters.

Stir the yogurt and vinegar into the remaining oil and lemon juice dressing until well blended. Season to taste.

Add the chicory/Belgian endive to the fennel in the bowl. Top with the beetroot/beets and herring and serve with the yogurt dressing.

Hash browns

2 tablespoons butter

1 onion, chopped

600 g/1¼ lbs. large
   potatoes, peeled and
   grated

1 egg white, beaten

vegetable oil,
   for deep-frying

sea salt and freshly ground
   black pepper

MAKES 16

These hash browns are deep fried, which means you probably won't be making them every day, but like fries, it's great to sometimes make your own. If you need to keep them warm while you cook the rest of your breakfast, pop them in the oven but put them on a wire rack first so they don't go soggy.

Heat the butter in a frying pan, then add the onion, cover with a lid and cook over low heat until soft.

Put the potatoes into a large mixing bowl and stir in the softened onions. Stir in the egg white and season generously.

Fill a large saucepan one-third full with vegetable oil. Heat to 190°C/375°F (or until a blob of the potato mixture browns within a few seconds).

Roll the potato mixture into walnut-sized balls, then flatten slightly before adding to the hot oil. Fry in batches of 4–5 for 2–3 minutes, until golden brown. Drain on kitchen paper/paper towels and serve with extra salt, for sprinkling.

Bacon & onion rösti

2 tablespoons unsalted
butter

1 onion, sliced

75 g/2½ oz. (smoked)
bacon, cubed

2 tablespoons chopped
fresh sage leaves

650 g/1½ lbs. Desiree/
Yukon gold potatoes,
peeled and grated

sea salt and freshly ground
black pepper

*20-cm/8-in. nonstick frying
pan*

SERVES 4

There is something very comforting about lovely crispy rösti. It makes a good side dish to grilled/broiled sausages too.

Melt half the butter in the frying pan over low heat. Add the onion and bacon, raise the heat to medium and cook for 7–8 minutes, until soft and lightly browned. Stir in the sage, then tip into a mixing bowl with the potatoes.

Add the remaining butter to the pan. When it stops foaming, spread the potato mixture over the base of the pan and press down with the back of a spatula. Fry for 6–7 minutes without moving it. When it's golden underneath, flip it over and cook for the same amount on the other side too.

Baked beans with maple syrup & paprika

2 x 400-g/14-oz. cans
  haricot/soldier, white
  navy or pinto beans, or
  400 g/14 oz. dried beans
2 tablespoons butter
250 g/8 oz. (streaky) bacon
  or pancetta
2 onions, chopped
1 teaspoon smoked
  paprika
2 teaspoons Dijon mustard
1 tablespoon tomato purée
250 ml/1 cup hot stock
6 tablespoons maple syrup
sea salt and freshly ground
  black pepper

SERVES 4

These homemade baked beans are utterly delicious. They are sweet and smoky and so irresistible. I like them piled on toasted and buttered whole-grain bread, or served with some hash browns if I am feeling really naughty.

If using dried beans, put them in large bowl. Add enough water to cover by 8 cm/3 inches and let stand overnight. The next day, drain the beans and put them in a saucepan of water. Bring to the boil and simmer for 40 minutes until tender. Drain.

Preheat the oven to 150°C (300°F) Gas 2.

Heat the butter in a large ovenproof casserole dish and fry the bacon until it has browned. Add the onions, paprika and mustard. Reduce the heat to low, cover with a lid and cook for 5 minutes, stirring occasionally, until it smells irresistible.

Add the cooked or canned beans, tomato purée, stock and some seasoning. Cover with a lid and bake in the preheated oven for 2 hours.

Give everything a good stir, add the maple syrup and taste to check the seasoning. Bake for a further 20 minutes with the lid off until the sauce has thickened. Serve with hot buttered toast or Hash Browns (see page 126).

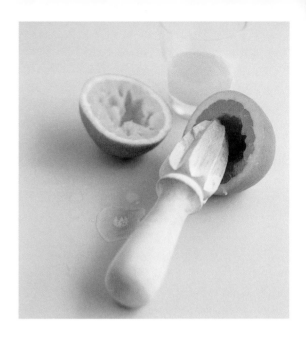

Bacon rolls with chilli & pecans

¼–½ teaspoon hot
   chilli powder
2 tablespoons demerara
   sugar
3 tablespoons shelled
   pecans
250 g/8 oz. (streaky) bacon
   slices
MAKES 16

These little rolls make a great change to regular crispy fried bacon. They are sweet but also have a fiery kick and a crisp texture from the chopped nuts.

Preheat the oven to 200°C (400°F) Gas 6.
   Put the chilli powder, sugar and pecans in a food processor and briefly blend until chopped but still coarse. Lay the slices of bacon on a baking sheet and scatter a little of the ground mixture over them. Roll up each rasher and scatter a little more of the ground mixture over the top of each roll. Bake in the preheated oven for 15 minutes, until crisp.

Roasted balsamic tomatoes

6 plum tomatoes
2 teaspoons (caster) sugar
sprig of fresh thyme,
   leaves only
2 tablespoons olive oil
2 tablespoons balsamic
   vinegar
sea salt and freshly ground
   black pepper
SERVES 4

Roasted tomatoes make a lovely change from fried tomatoes. They go really well with Hash Browns (see page 126) or the Bacon Rolls above, but you could just as easily eat them cold in salads.

Preheat the oven to 150°C (300°F) Gas 2.
   Slice the plum tomatoes in half lengthways and arrange, cut side up, on a baking sheet. Scatter over the sugar, thyme, oil and vinegar and season. Roast in the preheated oven for 1 hour, until they have lost some of their juiciness. Turn off the oven. Let them cool in the oven if there is time (to concentrate the flavours even further) or serve hot.

Bacon rolls with chilli & pecans, and Roasted balsamic tomatoes (left)

preserves

Peanut butter Plum kernel jam **Rhubarb & ginger jam** Passion fruit
curd Grapefruit & cardamom marmalade **Strawberry jam** White
chocolate praline spread

Peanut butter

300 g/2 cups shelled
    natural peanuts
2 teaspoons sea salt
5 tablespoons groundnut
    oil
2 tablespoons clear honey
1 or 2 large baking sheets
2 x 200-ml/half-pint jam jars,
    sterilized (see page 4)
**MAKES 2 X 200-ML/ HALF-
    PINT JARS**

**Why I've never thought about making my own peanut butter mystifies me.
It is so easy and so much better than the bought variety. You can make it with
cashew nuts and almonds too, which would make fabulous gifts.**

Preheat the oven to 180°C (350°F) Gas 4.

Put the peanuts, salt and 1 tablespoon of the oil in a large freezer bag and seal. Toss until the nuts are well coated. Tip out onto large baking sheets, making sure the nuts are in a single layer. Roast in the preheated oven for 6–8 minutes, until lightly golden. Stir halfway through. Remove from the oven and let cool.

Put the nuts in a food processor and blend until roughly chopped. Remove a third of the nuts now if you want crunchy peanut butter. Add the honey to the remaining paste, scrape down the edges of the bowl with a spatula and blend again. Trickle in the remaining oil and keep blending until you have a very smooth, spreadable paste. Fold in the reserved chopped nuts. Transfer to the sterilized jars and use within 3 weeks.

Plum kernel jam

750 g/1¾ lbs. (about 11)
    plums, halved
750 g/3¾ cups preserving
    or granulated sugar
300 ml/1¼ cups boiling
    water
freshly squeezed juice
    of ½ lemon
½ tablespoon unsalted
    butter
4–5 x 325-ml/half-pint jam
    jars, sterilized (see page 4)
waxed paper discs,
    to fit your jam jars
**MAKES 4–5 X 325-ML/
    HALF-PINT JARS**

**The kernels hidden inside plum stones/pits give off an ambrosial aroma. I am
lucky enough to have a plum tree so I have become very adept at this jam.**

Remove the stones/pits from the plums. Pop the stones/pits in a freezer bag and whack with a rolling pin until the stones/pits break and release the kernel. You only need 6 kernels, so discard the rest. Put the plums and sugar in a large, non-metal bowl, cover and leave overnight.

The next day, pop 2 or 3 saucers in the fridge. Put the reserved plum kernels in a large preserving pan (or non-aluminium saucepan) with the boiling water and lemon juice and bring back to the boil. Add the plums and sugar and cook for 20 minutes, or until they collapse. Squash them with the back of a spoon to help break up any large pieces, if necessary.

Raise the heat and boil for about 20–25 minutes, or until setting point has been reached – a sugar thermometer should read 105°C (220°F). To test for set, put ½ teaspoon of the jam on a chilled saucer, return it to the fridge or freezer for about 30 seconds or until cold, then prod the top. If a skin has formed, the jam is set. If not, return to the heat to cook for a little longer.

Stir in the butter to disperse any scum. Let cool for about 20 minutes, then transfer to the sterilized jars (wiping off any drips). Cover with waxed discs and seal with the lids while still warm. Label with the date and store in a cool, dark place for up to 6 months.

Peanut butter and Plum kernel jam (right)

Rhubarb & ginger jam

Rhubarb has that unique slightly metallic tang to it that you either love or loathe. I happen to love it and adore a jam made from it. Ginger and rhubarb have a natural affinity, but the vanilla helps to soften the flavours.

750 g/2 lbs. rhubarb,
 trimmed
750 g/4 cups granulated
 sugar
freshly squeezed juice
 of 2 lemons
5 cm/2 in. fresh ginger,
 bruised
1 vanilla pod/bean,
 halved lengthways
3–4 x 300-ml/half-pint jam
 jars, sterilized (see page 4)
waxed paper discs,
 to fit your jam jars
**MAKES 3–4 X 300-ML/
HALF-PINT JARS**

Chop the rhubarb into 5-cm/2 inch lengths and drop into a non-metal bowl with the sugar. Cover and leave overnight.

The next day, pop 2 or 3 saucers in the fridge.

Transfer the rhubarb mixture to a large preserving pan (or non-aluminium saucepan) with the lemon juice and ginger. Scrape the seeds out of the vanilla pod/bean and add to the pan along with the pod/bean halves. Bring to the boil, then cook over low heat until the sugar has dissolved. Raise the heat and boil for about 15–30 minutes – the timing will depend on whether you are using delicate forced rhubarb or tougher green rhubarb – or until setting point has been reached. A sugar thermometer should read 105°C (220°F). To test for set, put ½ teaspoon of the jam on a chilled saucer, return it to the fridge or freezer for about 30 seconds or until cold, then prod the top. If a skin has formed, the jam is set. If not, return to the heat to cook for a little longer.

Let cool for about 10 minutes, then fish out the ginger and vanilla pod/bean and discard. Transfer to the sterilized jars (wiping off any drips). Cover with waxed discs and seal with the lids while still warm. Label with the date and store in a cool, dark place for up to 6 months.

Passion fruit curd

150 ml/²/₃ cup passion fruit
  pulp (from about 6 fruit)
freshly squeezed juice
  of 1 lemon
3 whole eggs
3 egg yolks
100 g/½ cup golden caster
  sugar
100 g/7 tablespoons
  unsalted butter, chilled
  and cubed
2 x 250-ml/half-pint jam jars,
  sterilized (see page 4)
waxed paper discs,
  to fit your jam jars

**MAKES 2 X 250-ML/ HALF-
PINT JARS**

If you're a fan of lemon curd, then you will adore this. It is a little more perfumed than its lemony relative and somewhat sweeter. It goes brilliantly on any kind of bread or scone.

Bring a saucepan of water to the boil.

Take a heatproof bowl that will sit over your pan of boiling water. Sift the passion fruit pulp into the bowl and add the lemon juice, all the eggs and the sugar. Whisk until well mixed and set the bowl over the top of the pan of boiling water. Reduce the heat to low. Continue to whisk the mixture every 30 seconds, until it thickens. This should take about 10–15 minutes. Turn the heat off and add the cubed butter, whisking it in until the curd thickens.

Remove from the heat and continue to whisk until the mixture has cooled down. Transfer to the sterilized jars. Label with the date and keep refrigerated for up to 2 weeks.

Grapefruit & cardamom marmalade

2 grapefruits

4 lemons

about 900 g/4½ cups
    preserving sugar, or
    more

12 cardamom pods,
    crushed and seeds
    reserved

30-cm/12-in. square of
    muslin/cheesecloth

5–6 x 350-ml/half-pint jam
    jars, sterilized (see page 4)

waxed paper discs,
    to fit your jam jars

**MAKES 5–6 X 350-ML/
HALF-PINT JARS**

This is a very practical, easy way of making marmalade. The nonsense with muslin/cheesecloth jelly bags is simplified to make your life easier. The only thing you want to remember is you need to start the process a day early to give it time to extract the pectin. I love the tang of cardamom, which adds an unexpected level of flavour, but leave it out if you prefer.

Wash the grapefruits. Finely grate the zest, then wrap it up well with clingfilm/plastic wrap and set aside until you need it the next day.

Halve the lemons and squeeze the juice into a large non-metal bowl, adding the pips. Halve the naked grapefruits and squeeze the juice into the bowl, discarding the pips. Chop up the lemon and grapefruit shells and add to the bowl with 2 litres/2 quarts water. Cover with a clean tea towel/kitchen towel and leave in a cool place overnight.

The next day, pop 2 or 3 saucers in the fridge. Put the contents of the bowl into a large preserving pan (or non-aluminium saucepan) and bring to the boil over medium heat. Cover with a lid, then let simmer for about 1 hour.

Remove from the heat and let cool slightly. Line a sieve/strainer with your square of muslin/cheesecloth and set the sieve/strainer over a large bowl. Pour the mixture through to strain out the solids. Press down on the cooked fruit shells to

extract as much juice as possible, then discard them. Measure the juice (you should have about 1.25 litres/5 cups), then weigh out the correct amount of sugar: there should be a ratio of 450 g/2¼ cups sugar to 500 ml/2 cups juice.

Pour the juice back into the pan and bring to the boil. Add the weighed sugar, cardamom seeds and grapefruit zest and boil for 20–25 minutes, or until setting point has been reached – a sugar thermometer should read 105°C (220°F). To test for set, put ½ teaspoon of the jam on a chilled saucer, return it to the fridge or freezer for about 30 seconds or until cold, then prod the top. If a skin has formed, the jam is set. If not, return to the heat to cook for a little longer.

Let cool for about 20 minutes, then transfer to the sterilized jars (wiping off any drips). Cover with waxed discs and seal with the lids while still warm. Label with the date and store in a cool, dark place for up to 6 months.

Strawberry jam

900 g/2 lbs. slightly under-
ripe strawberries, hulled
and halved
750 g/3¾ cups preserving
or granulated sugar
freshly squeezed juice
of 1 lemon
½ tablespoon butter
2 x 325-ml/half-pint jam jars,
sterilized (see page 4)
waxed paper discs,
to fit your jam jars
**MAKES 2 X 325-ML/ HALF-
PINT JARS**

Macerating strawberries in sugar overnight reduces the amount of cooking time, which in turn means that the strawberries aren't cooked to mush, but retain some of their texture. You have to really watch for the setting point rather than relying on timing, as strawberries vary in water content and the more watery they are, the more cooking they will need.

Put the strawberries and sugar in a large non-metal bowl. Cover and let macerate overnight.

The next day, pop 2 or 3 saucers in the fridge. Transfer the contents of the bowl to a large preserving pan (or non-aluminium saucepan) and set over very low heat to dissolve any remaining sugar. Add the lemon juice and bring to the boil. Cook for 8–25 minutes, depending on the water content of the strawberries, or until setting point has been reached – a sugar thermometer should read 105°C (220°F).

To test for set, put ½ teaspoon of the jam on a chilled saucer, return it to the fridge or freezer for about 30 seconds or until cold, then prod the top. If a skin has formed, the jam is set. If not, return to the heat to cook for a little longer.

Stir in the butter to disperse any scum. Let cool for about 20 minutes, then transfer to the sterilized jars (wiping off any drips). Cover with waxed discs and seal with the lids while still warm. Label with the date and store in a cool, dark place for up to 6 months.

White chocolate praline spread

50 g/⅓ cup shelled
almonds, chopped
200 g/6½ oz. white
chocolate, chopped
300 ml/1¼ cups double/
heavy cream
2 x 250-ml/half-pint jam jars,
sterilized (see page 4)
**MAKES 2 X 250-ML/ HALF-
PINT JARS**

This is so naughty, but it is great for special occasions. I stole the idea from a Belgian café where they had this on the table for children. My feeling was that adults should share in this joy too. The chocolate mixture is just like making truffles, except when you spread it on hot toast, it melts into every pore.

Put the almonds in a dry frying pan over medium heat and let them heat up. Stir so they brown evenly, then remove from the heat.

Put the chocolate and cream in a heatproof bowl over a saucepan of gently simmering water. Do not let the base of the bowl touch the water and keep the heat low because white chocolate has a

tendency to split. Let melt for 5 minutes. Remove from the heat and stir until smooth. Add the toasted almonds and fold through.

Remove the bowl from on top of the pan and let cool completely. Transfer to the sterilized jars and refrigerate for up to 1 week. Bring to room temperature before eating.

Strawberry jam (left)

index

author's acknowledgements

A heartfelt thanks to the whole team at Ryland Peters & Small: to Céline for her eagle eye and Megan for her creative eye, as well as Alison for giving me this project in the first place. It has been a lifetime in the making, as breakfast has always been my favourite part of the day. Thanks to my wonderful, ever-reliable assistant Vorney for ploughing through all the recipes with me in my kitchen and then again on the shoot. To Jonathan and Liz, what can I say? Your collaboration on this project has created the most beautiful breakfast and brunch book I have ever set eyes on. You are amazing! And lastly but by no means least, huge gushes of love to my husband and family who encourage and inspire me every day.